COLORADO DISASTERS

TRUE STORIES OF **CENTENNIAL STATE** TRAGEDIES AND TRIUMPHS

PHYLLIS J. PERRY

FARCOUNTRY
PRESS

DEDICATION

For Casey, Clare, Julia, Emberline, and Katherine.

ACKNOWLEDGMENTS

WITH SPECIAL THANKS TO DAVID, WHO MAKES ALL THINGS POSSIBLE, to Jill Fernandez for technical and legal insights, to Claudia Mills, who cheers me on, and to my editor, Will Harmon, a word wizard, for his patience, skill, encouragement, and attention to detail throughout the writing of this book.

ISBN: 978-1-56037-810-5

© 2022 by Farcountry Press
Text © 2022 by Phyllis J. Perry

Front cover: Crews battle the Pine Gulch Fire.
Photograph courtesy of the Grand Junction Field Office, U.S. Bureau of Land Management.

Back cover: Floodwaters course through downtown Pueblo.
Photograph by Theodore Anderson, courtesy of the Denver Public Library,
Western History Collection, Z-5015.

Firestone house fire photographs on page 85 by Dennis Herrera, © Neo's Photography.

For more information about our books, write Farcountry Press,
P.O. Box 5630, Helena, MT 59604; call (800) 821-3874;
or visit www.farcountrypress.com.

Cataloging-in-Publication Data on file.

Produced and printed in the United States of America.

26 25 24 23 22   1 2 3 4 5 6

CONTENTS

REMEMBERING LIVES LOST AND LESSONS LEARNED

EVERY STATE SUFFERS THROUGH DISASTERS THAT ARRIVE IN VARIOUS forms, some peculiar to the local weather or geology, others more universal. In any given disaster, it may appear that the forces of nature need no additional help from humans to wreak their havoc. An earthquake, for example, or a flash food, hailstorm, or tornado strikes and causes great devastation. At other times, disasters take the combined efforts of nature and humans, such as when gases accumulate in a coal mine and then ignite and explode at the strike of a miner's match. And sometimes a momentary lapse of attention or a simple miscalculation by one person can trigger a disaster that might otherwise have been easily averted. On occasion, a disaster can be traced back to greed, fear, or hatred. Less frequently in our age of forensic science and litigious investigation, a disaster unfolds from causes that remain mysterious, unexplainable.

Landscape and weather often play outsized roles in the stories on the following pages, and it's not surprising that Colorado's mountains, forests, plains, and river canyons serve as much more than just a backdrop to the action. Avalanches, rockfalls, and landslides occur in the mountains, floods intensify in narrow canyons, and tornadoes sweep across open prairies where opposing weather systems clash.

These myriad forms of disaster may cause the loss of many lives, or they may not result in a single death but take a heavy toll in millions of dollars in lost property, livestock, or crops. As our landscape becomes more developed, monetary losses trend higher and higher. And as the news cycle has gone from weekly to daily to 24/7, we've come to expect the story to spotlight not only the victims but the heroes and villains as well. In fact, however intriguing the mechanical details of a disaster may be, it's the human element—the raw emotions, the decisive or panicked behavior, and often the selfless courage—that makes these stories so compelling.

This book delves into a range of selected disasters that reverberate through Colorado history. Rather than disgorge an exhaustive tally of every incident, this book presents a handpicked selection of disasters that shaped Colorado's topography, industries, public policies, and culture. A few notable disasters are absent from these pages. For example, an 1875 locust cloud of biblical proportions known as Albert's Swarm (as many as 12.5 trillion bugs in a mass covering more than 198,000 square miles) didn't kill anyone but ate every green thing in its path and unnerved the citizenry. And in 2015, a toxic-waste spill at the abandoned Gold King Mine north of Silverton sent a neon-orange plume down Cement Creek and the Animas River, eventually poisoning drinking and agricultural water in three states and the Navajo Nation. These catastrophes didn't make it into the following pages, not because they weren't significant or traumatic for the people affected, but simply because a book has a finite number of pages. Perhaps those stories will appear in volume two.

Whatever the type or cause, these disasters have altered Colorado's history, shaping the rise and decline of cities, transportation routes, energy and resource development, and public policy. In some cases, people have learned from the past and taken steps to prevent or at least minimize similar destruction and suffering. In others, we seem bent on ignoring the risks and repeating our mistakes. Either way, these cautionary tales are equally engaging and thought-provoking. Read these stories of tragedy, heroism, and generosity, and you will find yourself more informed, better prepared to face calamity, and perhaps inspired to be a helping hand when the time comes.

CHAPTER 1

FLOODS

COLORADO, AND PARTICULARLY THE FRONT RANGE, SITS AT AN atmospheric crossroads, where warm fronts from the south laden with moisture from the Gulf of Mexico regularly bump into cold fronts from the west and north. Such collisions can produce biblical amounts of precipitation and subsequent flooding. A sudden downpour may send a flash flood crashing down an otherwise dry gulch, and a days-long deluge might swamp an entire region. Both can cause catastrophe. Beyond the major floods described in this chapter, heavy precipitation plays a role in several other disasters covered in later chapters (see Train Wrecks, Blizzards and Avalanches, Rockfalls and Landslides, Airplane Crashes, and Massive Car Pileups).

GREAT FIRE AND FLOOD IN DENVER, 1863–1864

It may seem strange to start a chapter on floods with a story about a fire, but in this case one followed directly on the heels of the other.

Denver City was founded in 1858 at the confluence of Cherry Creek and the South Platte River. At first, it was little more than a tent city with a few hastily erected wooden buildings, but it grew rapidly. In its early years there was no fire department, so Denver citizens had to rely on volunteers when a fire broke out. Fire was a worry because most of the buildings were made of native pine, which contained a lot of highly flammable resin. Many buildings were packed close together. Most were a single story with false fronts to make them look taller than they were, but some were two-story

1

buildings. Even the homes of wealthier citizens had wooden frameworks. All of the buildings had wooden shingles. The city's brothels were particularly prone to fires, and rumor was that these were deliberately set to protest Denver's widespread prostitution industry.

By 1863, the city council had enacted basic fire regulations: no more wooden buildings could be built, stoves and fireplaces had to be inspected, and hay could not be stored within forty feet of structures. The council also passed a law that anyone who encountered a fire had to help put it out or incur a fine of $5. William N. Byers, founder and editor of the *Rocky Mountain News*, wrote often in his newspaper of the need for a professional fire department. The city council finally purchased a hook-and-ladder wagon and trained two bucket brigades.

As seen here in 1863, Denver was a small but growing town, with closely spaced wooden and brick buildings. PHOTOGRAPH BY WILLIAM G. CHAMBERLAIN, COURTESY OF THE DENVER PUBLIC LIBRARY, WESTERN HISTORY COLLECTION, X-19625.

In February 1863, a large fire broke out around midnight, and it took several hundred men to put it out. They were lucky there was no wind to fan the flames. The *Weekly Commonwealth and Republican* newspaper opined that on a windy night, such a fire would destroy every house in Denver. It was a prescient bit of prose.

At 2 A.M. on April 19, 1863, the wind was howling through Denver. It drowned out the sounds of revelry in the bars along Blake Street.

The wind even drowned out the first cries of "Fire!" after someone kicked over a stove in the Cherokee House saloon and hotel. A few people woke to fight the blaze, but the majority of the city's citizens didn't realize what was happening until they woke the next morning and found that a fair portion of downtown was now a pile of ashes.

The wind that was blowing so hard the night of the blaze came steadily from one direction, confining the fire to the east side of Cherry Creek. The trained fire brigade and volunteers tried to work together, chopping down wooden buildings in the path of the fire and storing some goods in the safety of the creek bed. But their efforts were disorganized, and the volunteers, though eager to help, were always in the way. Buckets of water slowed the flames a little, but it didn't take long for four blocks of the downtown area to burn to the ground.

The fire caused between $250,000 and $350,000 in damage, which would be several million dollars today. Seventy structures and 115 businesses were destroyed. Many people were left homeless, but no one was killed. Supplies of flour and sugar lost in the blaze became scarce, and their prices doubled.

In response to the fire, the city council enacted several new ordinances the very next day. The "brick ordinance" required that new buildings in the city be made of brick or stone. This ordinance remained in effect until the 1960s. Local brick makers increased production to meet the higher demand, and they made huge profits.

After the fire, rebuilding began immediately. Several businesses reopened a few days later in temporary structures, mostly tents. Most of the burned buildings had been uninsured, but funds were available for rebuilding. The Kountze brothers' bank had burned down, but it was quickly replaced by a new brick building, and this bank made loans to those who were also in the rebuilding process.

The *Rocky Mountain News* office had burned to the ground, so William Byers built his new office on stilts in the middle of Cherry Creek's streambed. Local Arapaho tribal members told Byers that this was a bad idea because Cherry Creek sometimes flooded. Byers ignored their advice, probably because he wanted both Auraria and Denver City residents to think of his paper as their hometown newspaper. By building his offices in the middle of the creek, he wasn't favoring either town site. Denver City and Auraria soon joined together to become one city, and following Byers' example, the new city hall and jail were also built on stilts in the Cherry Creek bed.

After the 1863 fire, many businesses, including the *Rocky Mountain News* (far right), rebuilt on stilts in the bed of Cherry Creek. PHOTOGRAPH BY HARRY M. RHOADS, COURTESY OF THE DENVER PUBLIC LIBRARY, WESTERN HISTORY COLLECTION, RH-233.

Not long after the merger of the two municipalities, Byers began to worry. Heavy rains on Palmer Divide to the south caused a modest rise in Cherry Creek, the headwaters of which rise there, about fifty miles south of downtown Denver. Byers published his concerns, writing, "Cherry Creek appears to present a rather serious problem, for we have had a demonstration of what may be expected from a heavy rainfall on the Divide, though we are not yet inclined to believe the Indian claims that the whole settlement is subject to flood."

The years before had been dry, but the spring of 1864 was especially wet. In the week leading up to May 19, rain fell steadily for several days, and, at one point, hailstones "as large as hens' eggs" hammered down for an hour in the mountains and on the prairie near Denver. Farmers had already lost sheep and cattle to the harsh weather, but people didn't worry about any danger from Cherry Creek, which was usually dry. Even when Cherry

4

and Plum Creeks began flowing higher than usual, no one raised any alarm. Then, a few minutes before midnight on May 19, a great wall of water carrying trees on its crest came hurtling down Cherry Creek. Witnesses reported that the flash flood roared as it went by, and some estimated that the crest of water was thirty feet high. It plowed into low-lying bridges that connected Auraria on the southwest bank and Denver City on the northeast bank, and floodwaters roiled against the bridge abutments and beams spanning the channel. The town of Auraria—what is today the Auraria Campus—was completely under water.

Cherry Creek reached a maximum sustained height of about twenty feet at 2 A.M. and began to ebb by 7 A.M. on May 20. The surging waters swept several bridges and many buildings off their foundations, including a large Methodist church and the *Rocky Mountain News* offices. Five *Rocky* employees were asleep in the building, but they awoke just in time to leap from a window into the relatively calm water of an eddy and swim to shore and safety.

The flood also carried away city hall, along with all the city and property records. The jail also collapsed, but not before prisoners were freed. One prisoner fell into the torrent; he clung to a log and was carried downstream until rescuers fished him out and saved him from drowning. Another man rode the roof of the jail like a raft on the current for three miles before being rescued.

All along Cherry Creek and down the South Platte River, businesses, horse stables, and homes were swept away. Whole sections of Denver were submerged in water five feet deep or more. Union soldiers from nearby Camp Weld built makeshift boats and began to rescue people stranded by the flood, including William Byers and his family, who were at their farmhouse outside of town. Along with his newspaper building, the flood took the Byers home, too, sweeping it from its foundations to an island on higher ground.

In the days following the flood, O. J. Goldrick, a writer for the *Rocky Mountain News*, covered the disaster in detail. With the *Rocky* offices demolished, Goldrick's report appeared instead in the *Weekly Commonwealth and Republican*. He described the scene in purple prose, writing, "It was the

Bystanders watch floodwaters surge through Denver, 1864. PHOTOGRAPH BY GEORGE D. WAKELY, COURTESY OF THE LIBRARY OF CONGRESS, LC-USZ62-5349.

water engine of death dragging its destroying train of maddened waves, that defied the eye to number them, which was rushing down upon us. . . . Alarm flew around and all alike were ignorant of what to think, or say, or do, much less of knowing where to go with safety or to save others. . . . Higher, broader, deeper, and swifter boiled the waves of water, as the mass of flood, freighted with treasure, trees, and live stock, leaped towards the Blake street bridge, prancing with the violence of a fiery steed stark mad."

The 1864 flood left many people homeless and sheltering temporarily in tents and wagons. Mud, debris, and ponds of contaminated water covered acres of once-productive land. In all, as many as twenty people lost their lives. Many head of livestock drowned, and property damages were estimated at $250,000 to $1 million, with the greatest destruction occurring in the low-lying section of Auraria.

Prices for food and supplies skyrocketed. Nevertheless, Denver quickly began to rebuild. New buildings went up in the eastern part of the city, and no more buildings were erected in the middle of Cherry Creek.

The creek has flooded since, however. In August 1933, Castlewood Dam failed and unleashed a seventeen-foot wall of water that overflowed Cherry Creek's incised channel into downtown. And in June 1965, torrential rains sent a wall of water down Plum and Cherry Creeks, once again flooding downtown Denver. In this case, Cherry Creek Reservoir (completed in 1950) caught its share of the water, while floodwaters surged down Plum Creek and into the South Platte, inundating parts of Denver once again.

GREAT PUEBLO FLOOD, 1921

The city of Pueblo straddles the Arkansas River at its confluence with Fountain Creek; both are welcome sources of water in the surrounding semiarid desert on the western edge of the Great Plains. First a trading post and then an agricultural hub, Pueblo boomed during the Colorado gold rush and soon became a center of the state's coal and steel industry, annexing the adjacent towns of South Pueblo, Central Pueblo, and Bessemer. In the early 1900s, you could get free passage to Pueblo from many countries around the world if you agreed that, on arrival, you would work in the steel mills. The immigrants who took advantage of this opportunity supplied the labor for the largest steel mills west of the Mississippi. In 1920, Pueblo was the second-largest city in Colorado, and the federal census counted 43,050 residents, many of whom were immigrants from Europe, the Philippines, and Mexico, drawn to jobs at the steel mills and railyards.

In an average year, Pueblo receives about twelve inches of precipitation, about two-thirds of which fall as rain. The mountains north and west of town tend to comb more moisture from the skies, and the area had seen occasional flooding in the past. In 1894, the Arkansas River overflowed its banks, prompting the city to widen the channel and build levees. Those measures, however, would prove to be insufficient.

June 1921 started out wetter than usual, with daily cloudbursts from an early onset of the summer monsoons. A high-pressure system to the north and low-pressure cell funneling moisture from the Gulf of Mexico collided and stalled over Pikes Peak and the upper Arkansas River basin.

Isolated heavy rains pounded the mountains and foothills surrounding Pueblo, saturating the soil, while the city itself recorded about 2 inches of rain on June 2 and 1.64 inches on June 3. Between June 3 and June 4, a total of 6 inches of rain fell.

The Arkansas River rose throughout the day on June 3, fed by heavy downpours in the mountains and hills. By 6 P.M., officials issued a flood warning, and by 7 P.M. the Arkansas River was eight feet above its normal flow. Unfortunately, the flood warning had the opposite of its intended effect—citizens ran to the riverbanks, in the words of one eyewitness, "thrilled at the angry high water." Within hours of the start of the storm, the floodwater in much of Pueblo's business district was ten feet deep.

At the railroad depot, slightly downslope from the river, two passenger trains half-filled with people sat waiting to depart. Crews decided to move the trains to higher ground on the far side of the river, but muddy floodwaters were already pushing against the bridge deck. Uprooted trees and other debris bashed into the span's supports. Rather than risk crossing the bridge, the engineers of both trains decided to return to the low-lying depot.

Then, at 8:45 P.M., the roiling river overtopped the levees. Josephine Pryor, the day manager of the telephone switchboards in the Pueblo Mountain States Telephone and Telegraph Company, had just gone off duty and walked home. Realizing the flood danger, she returned to the office on D Street. There, a young employee named Byron Thady was desperately working to save company records by carrying boxes of paper documents out of the flooding first floor. He continued his efforts while Pryor organized the thirty telephone operators on duty.

Pryor directed the women to call every subscriber downstream and in the rural areas and warn them to seek high ground. When the lights failed, Thady soaked rags in oil to create makeshift lamps to provide some light. Finally, the telephone operators lost electrical power. They watched water creep up the stairs to where they gathered on the second story of the building. Thady helped the women retreat to the third story. There they huddled and spent the night. When the garage next to their building was swept away, they heard and felt the lurch. A few men in a boat finally brought them slim rations, but the water was too turbulent to attempt to rescue the women.

On the morning of June 4, 1921, floodwaters coursed through the intersection of Main Street and Union Avenue in downtown Pueblo. PHOTOGRAPH BY THEODORE ANDERSON, COURTESY OF THE DENVER PUBLIC LIBRARY, WESTERN HISTORY COLLECTION, Z-5015.

The torrent roared through town, smashing into homes, shoving some off their foundations. Downtown was inundated, as were the train depot, railyards, and lumber mill. People fled to higher ground, but many were caught in the surge. Some accounts peg the swollen river at more than twenty-seven feet above normal flow. When electricity went out, Pueblo was plunged into darkness except for occasional lightning flashes. Then an eerie glow moved through the flooded streets; somehow, logs from the lumberyard had caught fire and were floating through town. As they slammed into homes and businesses, the buildings caught fire. The water surrounding the burning buildings was so deep that fire teams could not get near enough to help.

As the sun rose on June 4, the citizens of Pueblo surveyed a surreal scene of destruction. The flood had covered an area of more than 300 square miles. Debris and the bodies of livestock and humans alike poked out of the mud that seemed to cover everything. The river had spread a mile wide through the main business district. At the train depot, multi-ton cars were toppled on their sides and

The raging waters easily toppled multi-ton train cars and iron bridges. PHOTOGRAPH COURTESY OF THE DENVER PUBLIC LIBRARY, SPECIAL COLLECTIONS, X-10690.

mangled. Across town, homes had washed away, and plumes of smoke rose from fires still burning. But all the heroic women in the telephone building had survived. Both Pryor and Thady were honored for risking their lives to help save others.

The local Elks Club became a temporary relief center, assisting as many as 3,000 people a day. A camp was also built nearby to house refugees. Within a few days, aid was also available from the Knights of Columbus, Red Cross, Salvation Army, and some military units.

As the waters receded, Pueblo residents began cleaning up the muck and debris. The *Pueblo Chieftain*, Red Cross, and Colorado Rangers (state troopers) each published lists of victims and missing persons, but no official death toll was ever compiled. One flood survivor, Cora Rockefeller, was quoted in the June 9, 1921, *Western Star* as saying, "Read the worst you can and believe it. . . . The newspaper writers with their facts cannot give you half the picture. No one can say with certainty whether 500 or 5,000 lost their lives. It probably will never be known." Historian Wade Broadhead supports Rockefeller's statement. "Probably a lot more people died in the Pueblo flood than will ever be documented," he said. "[Many] were undocumented immigrants. They couldn't speak English and whole families were washed away."

Search parties found some victims' bodies more than sixty miles downstream from town. In 2020, a Harvard graduate student, Jonathan Cohen, completed his master's thesis on the Great Pueblo Flood, concluding that at least 693 and perhaps as many as 935 people died that night.

In the days following the flood, Pueblo was placed under martial law. The sheriff's department deputized about 1,500 Pueblo residents to help military troops and Colorado Rangers secure the town and prevent looting. The city also worked with the Red Cross to register 3,222 families for emergency relief. Then the massive task of rebuilding began.

The flood had destroyed more than 600 homes, 159 businesses, 46 locomotives, and 1,274 railroad cars. Damages totaled $25 million in 1921 dollars. A U.S. Geological Survey report estimated that the maximum discharge at the peak of the flood was 103,000 cubic feet per second, more than two and a half times the Arkansas River's previous recorded peak. The 1921

Even aerial views, taken from an airplane, could not capture the extent of the flooding. These images show the receding Arkansas River and devastation to Pueblo's railyards and surrounding neighborhoods. PHOTOGRAPHS COURTESY OF THE LIBRARY OF CONGRESS, LC-DIG-ANRC-14054 AND LC-DIG-ANRC-14055.

high-water mark is still visible on some downtown buildings. Flooding also devastated the Arkansas Valley thirty miles upstream of Pueblo, all the way to the Kansas border.

Pueblo did rebuild, adding taller, more robust levees and stormwater drainage systems, but two steel mills shuttered later that year and business growth slowed. Unable to keep pace with Colorado Springs and Denver, Pueblo languished. Another major flood struck in 1965. Completion of the Pueblo Dam on the Arkansas River in 1975, six miles west of the city, improved flood protection, as well as provided hydropower and recreational opportunities. But portions of Pueblo still experience serious floods, including the Peppersauce Bottoms neighborhood, which was swamped as recently as 2006. Although the city has endured for more than a century, floods have scarred its landmarks, and residents know that the Arkansas River and Fountain Creek will rise again.

DENVER FLOOD, 1965

In the mid-1960s, after three years of drought, Coloradoans wanted rain, and when June 1965 arrived looking gray and dark with a promise of rain, no one complained. Then a cold front swept in from the northeast and met up over the Front Range with warm, humid air moving northward from the Gulf of Mexico. For several days, a bank of dark thunderheads cloaked the mountaintops. Then finally, the skies dropped heavy rain.

On June 14, a sudden hailstorm pelted southeast Colorado Springs. Fort Carson soldiers were called in to shovel tons of golf-ball-sized hailstones out of homes in Stratmoor Hills. To the north, funnel clouds were sighted, and a tornado in Loveland smashed cars and trees. The next day, rain and hail moved northward, hitting Greeley and Sterling before moving on to Nebraska. Hail fell so thick and so quickly that it clogged storm drains. Two tributaries of the South Platte River—Pawnee Creek and Lodgepole Creek—overflowed their banks, submerging roads in Logan and Sedgwick Counties. Some fields were under three feet of water; sheep and cattle drowned.

Floodwaters soon swamped four broad areas: north of Greeley and north and west of Sterling, the upper Plum Creek and Cherry Creek basins, the Kiowa and Bijou Creek basins, and along Plum Creek and the South Platte River from Plum Creek to North Platte, Nebraska.

On the early afternoon of Wednesday, June 16, heavy rains fell on the southern edge of Douglas County. A tornado tore through the small town of Palmer Lake, ripping the roofs off thirty houses. Scooping up water, gravel, and even fish and frogs from the nearby lake, the tornado then dropped this slurry into peoples' homes. Record-breaking torrential rain continued to fall. Fourteen inches of rain fell in just four hours in Larkspur and Castle Rock, as well as in Douglas County south of Castle Rock.

Another fourteen-inch, four-hour downpour drenched Dawson Butte, just north of Palmer Lake. Roads became rivers, and fields turned into lakes. It also poured on Raspberry Mountain, near Larkspur, about six miles south of Dawson Butte. Residents reported that they had never before seen rain that heavy. As the storm continued, the temperature dropped rapidly.

The rain and an overflowing East Plum Creek moved into Castle Rock. Boulders rumbled along the riverbed, and people heard trees snapping in the torrent. The floodwaters wiped out roads and bridges in their path. Telephone lines went down, and one firsthand account said that it was hard to breathe outdoors, like standing under a waterfall.

Just south of Castle Rock, fifteen-year-old Jim Lowell ventured out on his family ranch to see if he might rescue some of the animals in the barn, stranded in what now looked like a lake. As he approached the barn, the water was waist deep; it was slow going. Soon the water was up to his chest. Jim realized that he was no longer on a mission to rescue livestock; he needed to save himself. He climbed onto the barn roof, where he waited out the storm. He didn't know it then, but Jim certainly wasn't the only one to find himself stuck on a roof during the June flood.

The east and west branches of Plum Creek joined just outside of Sedalia and swept through the main street of town, flooding several homes, a church, and the grange hall. The creek, normally only a few feet wide, now spanned nearly a mile. It was hard to measure the force of the runoff because the gauging station at Louviers had washed away. But later calculations suggested that, in three hours, the flow of Plum Creek increased to forty times its usual flow. Buildings, trees, automobiles, and heavy construction equipment were swept away. Large quantities of gravel and sand, pulled from riverbanks and streambeds, were carried off and dumped downstream. One resident said, "The banks of the creek disappeared as if the land was made of sugar." This unfolding disaster was no longer considered simply a flood; it was now being called a 100-year flood.

State Patrol officers warned that a twenty-foot-high wall of water was coming down Plum Creek straight for Littleton, Englewood, and Denver, carrying cars, trees, and other debris. They estimated that it would hit Denver around 8 P.M. A second crest was not far behind. Police officers went door to door to homes along the river, urging occupants to flee to higher ground.

By the afternoon of June 16, the Denver Police Department had cleared its radio traffic for nothing but emergency calls. Police closed off all the bridges that spanned the South Platte River. Three bystanders watching a bridge being battered by huge piles of debris were swept into the river when the bridge collapsed. Luckily, the National Guard was able to rescue them. Catastrophe was narrowly averted when one piece of flotsam—a huge butane tank—barely cleared the Florida Avenue Bridge. Above the constant roar of grinding stones and debris, explosions cracked the evening and flames shot into the sky. Lights failed and the city grew dark as water swamped power plants. The Evans Avenue Bridge held through the night but collapsed two days later. The Colfax viaduct survived. In all, twenty-six bridges were washed away. Two butane tanks exploded at Sixth Avenue and Platte River Drive in a blast that could be heard for miles.

Two of the hardest hit areas were the Valverde and Athmar Park neighborhoods. The Valley Highway at Alameda was submerged, and the river spread out from Santa Fe Drive to Tejon Street. A floating boxcar crashed into a building on South Jason Street. Seven people were spotted on the roof of a nearby building that was surrounded by floodwater. The Denver fire chief and a fire captain set out in a rowboat to rescue them, but the boat capsized in the middle of Tejon Street. The current was too swift to swim against. The chief and captain kept afloat by holding on to debris in the river. It took another two hours for fire department members using another rowboat, powerboats, and ropes to rescue the chief and his captain from the water, as well as the seven citizens stranded on the roof of the building.

Just a few blocks away, Kenneth Fisher was helping his grandmother evacuate her building. As he got her safely settled, he heard a call for anyone with a boat to come and help. Someone was signaling for assistance from the top of a sign at the Gaslight Motel. Fisher headed in his motorboat for Alameda and Tejon, where he met up with two police officers. The three

Homes in the Valverde area were swamped by the flood. PHOTOGRAPH BY TERRY BRENNAN, COURTESY OF THE DENVER PUBLIC LIBRARY, SPECIAL COLLECTIONS, X-29250.

of them set out in the murky waters. The swift current and all kinds of debris made it difficult, but Fisher managed to get his boat close to the motel, and the policemen helped three stranded men down from the motel sign and into the boat. After safely depositing them on higher ground, Fisher and the police officers went back into the floodwater to save others, including a middle-aged couple and an older woman. The three were playing cards by candlelight in their flooded home. The police convinced them to leave through their second-story window, although the older woman was reluctant to go. The next morning they found that their home had washed away.

In metro Denver, the destruction was far greater than anything experienced before. The flood claimed twenty-one lives and was credited with another 327 injuries and illnesses. Property damage, adjusted for inflation, totaled over $4.5 billion in 2020 dollars.

The debris in the water was as bad or worse than the floodwater itself. Entire brick houses, foundations and all, came crashing down the river. Water engulfed the Centennial Racetrack, burying the stables in mud.

A concerted effort by owners, jockeys, and trainers managed to save more than 100 horses at the track, but at least another 100 horses died.

The following morning, the extent of the damage could be seen. In Denver, 67 percent of the flood damage was in the industrial area. Mud was everywhere. The floodwaters destroyed thousands of homes and businesses. Many farm animals drowned. Jim Lowell made it down safely from the barn roof on his ranch, but later his prize calf was found dead ten miles away. Business owners faced dealing with everything from warped bowling-alley lanes to soggy merchandise. For many, the worst losses were irreplaceable personal possessions.

Flooding inundated railyards along the South Platte River. PHOTOGRAPH BY GEORGE E. MEISTER, COURTESY OF THE DENVER PUBLIC LIBRARY, SPECIAL COLLECTIONS, Z-168.

As the flood pushed north, other tributaries added their waters to the flow: Sand Creek, Clear Creek, the Bijou, Little Beaver, and the Cache la Poudre River. The course of the South Platte all the way to the Nebraska border was filled with mud and wreckage. The water spread out over 250,000 acres of farmland, isolating communities such as Brush, Sterling, and Fort Morgan.

This 1965 flood was the impetus for finally completing a number of long-delayed flood-control projects in metro Denver. The existing infrastructure was inadequate. Castlewood Canyon Dam, built in the 1890s, had failed in 1933 during heavy rains and sent floodwaters toward Denver thirty-five miles away. Five thousand residents were evacuated. Cherry Creek Dam was completed in 1950. That same year, a proposed Chatfield Dam was authorized by Congress, but the project stalled. Property owners were not in favor of building a dam there, and there was little political interest in the project. There had been little flooding of the South Platte over the past century. The area was mostly filled with factories and railyards. It was a dumping ground for old cars and trash. There were hobo camps, and adjacent to the river were the city's poorest neighborhoods.

City officials and citizens finally focused their attention on the lack of planning and the haphazard building and neglect along creeks and rivers. Chatfield Dam was finally completed in 1972 by the U.S. Army Corps of Engineers.

Although improvements took several decades to complete, the floodplain along the South Platte River through Denver is no longer a dump but an area of flood mitigation and beautiful open space designed for recreation. Littleton passed a tax in 1971 to help pay for the creation of South Platte Park, now an 880-acre park along two and a half miles of riverfront. The nonprofit Gateway Foundation became a leading proponent for cleaning up and developing the South Platte River through Denver. Many of the projects are multi-use: for example, a pedestrian and bicycle trail can also serve as a flood-control maintenance road. Nature areas and over 100 miles of trails for hikers and bikers line the river. Out of the great Denver flood of 1965 has come not only the completion of many flood-control projects but a beautiful open-space corridor through the city.

BIG THOMPSON FLOOD, 1976

The headwaters of the Big Thompson River arise in Forest Canyon, within Rocky Mountain National Park. The river then runs east through Moraine Park to the town of Estes Park and to Olympus Dam, where it pauses in Lake Estes before hurrying into Big Thompson Canyon. A major tributary, the North Fork of the Big Thompson, begins on the northern slopes of the Mummy Range. The North Fork flows east through the town of Glen Haven and merges with the main Big Thompson at the town of Drake, in the canyon about thirteen river miles downstream from Estes Park. The Big Thompson emerges from the mountains west of Loveland and then flows east across the plains into Weld County, completing its seventy-eight-mile run as it joins the South Platte River south of Greeley.

At about 5 P.M. on Saturday, July 31, 1976, a light rain began to fall on the higher elevations of the Big Thompson basin. No one expected a major storm; the weather report for the day called for only a 40 to 50 percent chance of showers or thunderstorms, typical of the summer monsoon season. It was a holiday weekend; Sunday, August 1, marked the centennial of the Centennial State's entry into the Union as the thirty-eighth state. Campgrounds, motels, and summer cabins in the canyon were packed with 3,500 visitors for the three-day weekend.

But as the rain continued, it grew heavier. Instead of moving south to north, as most monsoonal storms do, this thunderstorm stalled and dumped its water over one area. Local residents along the Big Thompson reported seeing beach balls, small propane tanks, and lunch baskets floating by, all signs that the rain had disrupted holiday picnics upstream. By 9 P.M., light rain had moved into the lower portion of the canyon, but moderate rain was falling in Estes Park, and seriously heavy rain was hitting the higher elevations of the basin. Lightning flashed across the night sky, and people complained that it was difficult to breathe in the moisture-laden air. The warm rain came straight down in sheets—an estimated twelve inches in less than four hours. As all of this water collected in the river, it gained power and speed as it rushed downstream into the V-shaped canyon.

At about 8 P.M., the Colorado State Patrol first received word of rising water levels. There was no way to issue a mass warning to everyone living in Big Thompson Canyon—no master phone list, no siren system. Ham radio operators quickly connected the region's medical clinics, outlying helicopter pads, and an emergency command post at the Drake Store and then relayed messages to a central hub in Estes Park. But communication remained a challenge. Where possible, police officers went door to door to warn residents. Some people chose to evacuate, but many ignored the warnings. They reasoned that they had seen rising water in the canyon before, and it had always dropped back down without major damage. People were reluctant to leave the comfort of their homes in the rain in the middle of the night. With homes scattered all along the river, police were able to warn only about 20 percent of canyon residents.

Sergeant Willis Hugh Purdy, a twenty-six-year veteran of the state highway patrol who lived in Loveland, was home that evening watching the Olympic Games on television. His dispatcher called to relay a report of a rockslide on U.S. Highway 34 in Big Thompson Canyon. A second call came to advise him about a highway washout. Purdy pulled on a slicker and went to investigate. At the same time, Officer William Miller of the State Patrol was on U.S. Highway 36 south of Estes Park. Officer Tim Littlejohn, who was at the southern edge of Fort Collins, also hurried toward the canyon. Purdy radioed Littlejohn and told him to set up a roadblock at the bottom of the canyon and turn approaching motorists around. Purdy continued up the canyon, urging people along the way to evacuate. Miller, at the top of the canyon, radioed Purdy to report that the road was flooded, with water rising up to his car doors. He left his vehicle and climbed to safety. Purdy radioed from the vicinity of Drake about fifteen minutes later, saying he was stuck right in the middle of the flood and unable to get out. That was the last transmission anyone heard from Purdy.

Louise Dikeman and a friend were out enjoying the day with their four children when the rain began. They hurried back to their pickup truck and headed down U.S. Highway 34. But the river had already cut through the road ahead, and then the roadway behind them collapsed. They were trapped on a stretch of highway only eighteen feet long. The two women weighed whether to climb the mountainside with the kids and sit in the rain or stay in the truck. They decided to wait in the truck but spent the night watching the raging river tear away pieces of the roadway in front of and behind them. In the morning, a helicopter appeared and landed on the island of highway. The pilot had been told that Olympus Dam had broken and a flood surge was headed down the canyon. The helicopter had room for only one more passenger. Thinking that they all would soon die,

Dikeman handed her baby boy into the helicopter, fearing she might never see him again. The helicopter flew away, and Dikeman awaited her fate. But the report about the dam breaking was mistaken. Two park rangers arrived and rescued Dikeman, her friend, and the three remaining children. A relieved Dikeman was soon reunited with her son.

The Big Thompson River scoured its channel, undercutting banks and adjacent homes. PHOTOGRAPH BY RALPH R. SHROBA, COURTESY OF THE U.S. GEOLOGICAL SURVEY.

Few people realized the true nature of the flood. It started with a gradual rising of the river, but then a flash flood sent a twenty-foot-high wall of water surging down Big Thompson Canyon at fourteen miles per hour. The water picked up mud and debris, becoming a churning mass of trees, boulders, smashed buildings, and other flotsam.

Michel Conley, a thirty-year-old, off-duty Estes Park seasonal policeman, was traveling through the canyon when the flood hit. He sent his wife, Phyllis, to safety on higher ground and then helped others escape the rising waters. Conley rescued at least sixty people before being trapped himself by the raging river. He grabbed a pole to try to save himself, but it broke and Conley disappeared into the muddy water.

Leroy and Clara Graham were at home in Cedar Cove, downstream from Drake, when a call came about flooding upstream. The couple had moved to Colorado from Texas to retire in their mountain cabin near their son and his family. Clara went to warn neighbors, and Leroy, a volunteer firefighter, took the fire truck from the local station and began driving up the canyon. He passed the Loveland hydroelectric plant (near the site of today's Viestenz-Smith Mountain Park) and crossed a bridge over the river. Then a surge of floodwater struck the fire truck head on, spun it around, and flipped it onto its side. Graham managed to get out and climb a tree.

Meanwhile, back in Cedar Cove, the Grahams' son Bob had noticed the river coming up rapidly. He dragged a water pump away from the river's edge and then took a phone call from a friend, a Loveland firefighter, who asked how high the river was at Bob's house. While on the phone, Bob looked out a window at the river and saw a metal bridge just upstream come loose in the current. Bob dropped the phone and shouted to his wife, Beverly, "We need to get out now!" They grabbed their daughters—Teresa, nine, and Lisa, two—and ran to their car. But Bob turned back to grab some warmer clothes. Just as he reached the cabin, a huge surge of water hit, swallowing Beverly and the two girls. Bob pulled himself onto the cabin roof as another surge tore away half of the structure. "My parents had a cabin just two doors up from us," Bob remembered. "My mom made it to their car. I saw her looking out the window at me as her car washed away."

Bob spent most of the night on the roof, not knowing that his father, Leroy, was clinging to a tree up the canyon, or that he would never see his mother, Clara, or wife and children alive again. In the coming days, Clara's body would be found near Loveland, and Beverly and Lisa's bodies were recovered several miles downstream from Cedar Cove. Teresa was never found.

Other canyon residents were in similarly perilous situations. Some clung to trees or ledges on the steep canyon walls. Others cut holes through their ceilings and sat on mattresses on top of their roofs. Many houses floated in the raging river with people clinging to them. Eighteen helicopters battled rain and fog to pluck people out of danger, one by one. Rescuers dangled from ropes below the choppers to pick up people trapped on rooftops, riverbanks, and canyon walls. The crews worked throughout the night and into the next day, rescuing 800 people from the canyon. One of those crews was aboard a Flight For Life civilian helicopter. Established only four years earlier,

Flight For Life gained enormous experience in rescue operations that night. In a span of nineteen hours, that one crew rescued 150 people.

Fifteen-year-old Mary Myers was visiting her grandmother in Drake. The storm had knocked out power to town, and Mary and a friend named Amy sat at a window watching the frequent lightning. She noticed people with flashlights near the river and went out to investigate. Recalling the scene years later, Mary said, "As I neared the bridge, I heard the roaring water, looked upstream and saw the first wall of water tumbling down the river. It was illuminated from the inside from the cars whose lights had not yet shorted out. As the water crashed on the bridge, I was already running to the house to wake my grandmother."

The house was safely above the river, so Mary and Amy huddled on the porch and watched the flood through the night. At 3 A.M., a National Guard Chinook helicopter arrived and began airlifting people out of Drake. Mary stayed behind to help a neighbor couple who were disabled. They wouldn't leave without their five cats, so Mary helped them put the cats into a cardboard box. Then they all got on board the next Chinook. "The box was not secure enough to contain those panicked cats, and they got loose in the helicopter," Mary recalled. "That is the definition of chaos." She was soon reunited with her grandmother and Amy.

Vehicles washed away by the flood often ended up miles downstream, buried in mud or gravel.
PHOTOGRAPH BY WALLACE R. HANSEN, COURTESY OF THE U.S. GEOLOGICAL SURVEY.

Many people who tried to outrun the flood in their cars soon found the road covered in water or washed away. They abandoned their vehicles and climbed the canyon's steep slopes as far as they could. From their perches, they watched their cars disappear downstream in the raging torrent.

Driving a patrol car up from Loveland, two sheriff's deputies passed the hydroelectric plant above Cedar Cove and found that the brick building had washed away, leaving only the turbines and the concrete foundation. Just above the plant, the road had washed out. The deputies turned around and used a loudspeaker to urge people to get to higher ground. They also radioed reports back to headquarters. At dawn, they discovered a seventy-year-old man near the river buried waist-deep in silt. "Well, it's about time," the old man cried to his rescuers.

The storm eventually moved north, dumping heavy rain on the North Fork of the Big Thompson River near Glen Haven. Guests at the Glen Haven Inn were aware of the rain, and employees saw water seeping into the kitchen, but no one was especially worried. After the power went out, the guests sat around the piano and sang "Stormy Weather" and "Old Man River." In the morning, they realized that town hall, which was just across the street from them, had been swept off its foundation. The cars in the hotel parking lot were buried in silt up to their windows.

A local firefighter later recounted helping a woman evacuate from her home. The two drove away through the flood, but the vehicle fell into a huge hole filled with water. They clambered out, but the woman could not swim and almost drowned. She finally pulled herself out by clinging to bushes and then walked back home, where she safely spent the night.

As daylight broke and floodwaters receded, search teams combed the canyon looking for survivors and recovering bodies. In the coming days, homeowners returned to inspect their properties and begin the enormous task of cleaning up all the mud and debris. Many homes were simply gone; perhaps just a fireplace or foundation remained to show where the house had been. One resident found his cabin still on its foundation, but the flood had blown out all the doors and windows. The interior was filled with mud six feet deep. Throughout the canyon, cleanup and repairs would go on for months.

The flood carried whole houses downstream and twisted bridges off their piers. PHOTOGRAPH BY WALLACE R. HANSEN, COURTESY OF THE U.S. GEOLOGICAL SURVEY.

The streamflow at the mouth of Big Thompson Canyon on July 31, 1976, before the storm, was 165 cubic feet per second (cfs). The highest flow previously recorded there was 8,000 cfs, during a flood in 1919. The 1976 flood peaked at four times that amount, an astonishing 31,200 cfs.

In the final tally, the Big Thompson Flood destroyed 418 homes, 52 businesses, and 400 cars. Another 138 homes were damaged. Most of U.S. Highway 34 in the canyon was gone, along with numerous bridges. Damages totaled more than $30 million in 1977 dollars. In all, 143 people died, 5 of whom were never found, and 250 or more were injured. (For decades, the death toll stood at 144, but in 2008 Barb Anderson, a Big Thompson Canyon resident who organized an annual memorial for the flood victims, discovered that one presumed victim, Darrell Johnson, was alive and living in Oklahoma City. He did not know that he was on the list of victims. In July 1976, he and his family had rented a cabin at Sleepy Hollow resort, but they decided to cut their stay short and left just hours before the flood washed away the entire resort.)

Another significant flood hit the Big Thompson again in 2013, but the 1976 flood remains the deadliest natural disaster in Colorado history. A roadside memorial honors Sergeant Purdy and Officer Conley. Purdy likely saved hundreds of lives by warning people to evacuate as he drove up the canyon.

Canyon resident Barb Anderson organized an effort to erect a memorial near Drake with the names of all of the flood victims. For decades, she invited survivors and family members to gather there to remember their loved ones. The event was held yearly every July 31; eventually, as time passed, people began gathering every five years. The event features stories from survivors, singing, and a time of remembrance. Bob Graham rarely goes near the canyon, but he's attended the memorial ceremony and spoken of his experiences that night. Also, scholarships funded by donations and the sales of two books about the flood (including *Reflections of the Heart*, by Barb Anderson) are awarded to college students who lost parents, grand-parents, or great-grandparents that night in 1976.

Today, the roadway through the canyon runs higher above the river than it did in 1976. It's also dotted with signs reminding motorists of the flood hazard and to seek higher ground in the event of high water. Updated floodplain maps and regulations limit construction along the river. And weather forecasting technology has improved tremendously. "In 1976, data was old by the time we got it," said Nezette Rydell, lead forecaster with the National Weather Service's Denver-Boulder Forecast Office. Now, Doppler radar and weather satellites stand constant vigil, alerting meteorologists to any unusual weather patterns and developing storms. A repeat of 1976's deadly surprise is unlikely, but as the rains of 2013 proved, when storms threaten, it's wise to keep a wary eye on the Big Thompson.

LAWN LAKE DAM FAILURE, 1982

The Big Thompson Flood of 1976 was a natural disaster caused by heavy rain. Just six years later, another flood raged at the headwaters of the Big Thompson River, but this one was unleashed by human neglect.

One of the streams forming the Big Thompson's headwaters, the Roaring River, begins in Crystal Lake, an alpine tarn nestled below 13,508-foot Fairchild Mountain in the Mummy Range west of Estes Park. The stream trickles over bedrock benches for less than a mile to Lawn Lake, which sits right at tree line at an elevation of about 11,000 feet. Glacially formed and naturally dammed by a small terminal moraine, Lawn Lake had a surface area of 16.4 acres. Then in 1903, farmers with thirsty crops in the fields around Loveland formed an irrigation company to build an earthen embankment dam. This added seven feet to the height of the glacial moraine, for a total storage capacity of 498 acre-feet of water. In 1932, the dam was raised to twenty-six feet tall, increasing the lake's storage capacity to 817 acre-feet, or about 35 million cubic feet of water at full pool. From Lawn Lake, water flowed down the Roaring River to the Fall River, then to Estes Park and the Big Thompson, which carried it to the farmers' fields in Loveland. In 1915, Congress established Rocky Mountain National Park, encompassing Lawn Lake and the Roaring River drainage.

Lawn Lake is remote, high in the mountains, and access is challenging and seasonal. Over the years, the maintenance road to Lawn Lake fell into disrepair, eventually becoming impassable for vehicles. Workers had to hike six miles to reach the lake. Dam inspections grew infrequent, though reports did note concerns with the structure in 1951, 1975, 1977, and 1978. The last two inspection reports said the dam was in "fair" condition and suggested repairs, but none were made.

Then, on July 15, 1982, at about 6 A.M., the Lawn Lake Dam abruptly gave way, releasing 30 million cubic feet of water, enough to fill a sports stadium three times. A thirty-foot-high wall of water charged down the Roaring River valley, ripping out soil, trees, and boulders as it went. It's estimated that Lawn Lake emptied in about thirty minutes.

That same morning, Stephen Gillette, a driver for the A-1 Trash Company, had started his rounds through Rocky Mountain National Park an hour earlier than usual because mechanical troubles had prevented two trucks from completing their routes the day before. At about 6:15 A.M., Gillette pulled into the Lawn Lake trailhead parking lot, near where the Roaring River flows into the Fall River. He heard a "roaring sound," which at first he thought was a jet airplane close over-head. But then he saw ". . . a ponderosa pine, limbs, bark, and all, the whole thing, just sailing up, above the other trees. . . ." Gillette threw his truck into reverse and blocked the parking-lot entrance. Then he jumped out of the cab and used a nearby emergency phone, which happened to work that day despite being notoriously unreliable. The park dispatcher who answered heard a roar and Gillette shouting, "A lake, a dam— something's flooding!"

Two park rangers soon arrived, and they quickly locked the Fall River Road gate and barricaded Horseshoe Park Road to keep traffic well away from the floodwaters. In the time this took, the swollen river was up to their knees. The rangers knew they were dealing with a flood, but they had no idea why—it had not rained and the sky was clear. They also couldn't foresee how much worse the situation would quickly become.

One eyewitness later reported, "I started to hear a sound like an airplane. There were loud booms. It got louder and louder. I thought it was breaking the sound barrier. I kept looking for a plane but couldn't see one. I got suspicious and started to look upstream. I saw trees crashing over and a wall of water coming down." Another observer said, "It looked like a brown cloud and sounded like a freight train."

Two young friends from Wisconsin were camped that morning along the Roaring River. Steven See and Steven Cashman, both twenty-one, were enjoying a road trip to the Rocky Mountains. Their adventure was cut short when the river literally roared into their camp. Cashman managed to escape, but See was swept away, still in his sleeping bag.

As the Roaring River exited its steep, narrow canyon at Horseshoe Park, the torrent found room to spread out over more open terrain, depos-iting uprooted trees and boulders weighing as much as 452 tons. The flood created an alluvial fan of debris that today stretches across forty-two acres and is forty-four feet deep in places.

Though temporarily slowed, the muddy floodwaters continued carving their way to the Fall River and then downstream to Cascade Lake and its seventeen-foot-high, concrete dam. The small lake was quickly overwhelmed, and the flood surged over the top of the dam. The concrete held for about seventeen minutes.

Floodwaters overtopped and eventually collapsed Cascade Dam, shown here moments before the dam crumbled. PHOTOGRAPH COURTESY OF THE U.S. GEOLOGICAL SURVEY.

In the nick of time, park dispatch had sent a ranger to Aspenglen Campground, about half a mile below Cascade Dam. The ranger told campers at the walk-in tent sites closest to the Fall River that "it would be wise to evacuate." The water was muddy and rising, but the ranger did not warn campers that a dam had failed or that a flood was approaching. It's unclear whether the ranger himself understood the danger. Fortunately, campers heeded the warning and moved to higher ground. Two people, however, returned to the riverside sites.

Bridget Dorris, twenty, from Arlington, Texas, and Terry Coates, thirty-six, of Peoria, Illinois, were last seen crossing a footbridge over a channel of the Fall River. Coates, a public schoolteacher and administrator, had been camped at one of the riverside sites at Aspenglen with his wife, Rosemary, and their children: Marcian, nine, and Adam, five. The family hadn't heard the ranger's warning, but other campers had relayed the message. They quickly loaded their tent and camping gear into their car, and Terry grabbed his camera to photograph the rising river. Soon, Rosemary heard a noise upstream, saw a rush of water, and moved to higher ground with her children.

Cascade Dam had collapsed, creating a wall of water that destroyed Aspenglen Campground, carrying off tents, picnic tables, propane tanks, and cars—as well as Terry Coates and Bridget Dorris. The debris flow surged toward Estes Park.

Downstream from the campground, the flood demolished a state fish hatchery, including 90,000 fish, and then hit the Fall River Hydroplant, which had been built in 1909 by F. O. Stanley (maker of Stanley Steamer motorcars and owner of the famed Stanley Hotel in Estes Park). The torrent raced onward and reached the outskirts of Estes Park at 8:12 A.M.

Floodwaters funnel down Elkhorn Avenue in Estes Park. PHOTOGRAPH BY Z. BLEUINS, U.S. BUREAU OF RECLAMATION, COURTESY OF THE U.S. GEOLOGICAL SURVEY.

Dick McCracken, superintendent of the Estes Park water department, drove his truck down the town's main street, Elkhorn Avenue, just in front of the wall of water. Through a loudspeaker, he broadcast a final evacuation warning for anyone still in town. On McCracken's heels, the roiling flood tore up Fall River Road, wiping out bridges, and then hurtled down Elkhorn Avenue, sweeping homes and businesses off their foundations and filling others with water and mud. In all, the flood demolished or severely damaged 108 homes and 177 businesses (75 percent of all commercial properties in town). Particularly hard-hit were the Fall River Trailer Court, Nicky's Resort, and the Ponderosa Lodge. The shops on the south side of Elkhorn Avenue were hit hardest. The flood finally swirled to a stop on the east end of town in Lake Estes, held by the steel-girded Olympus Dam.

Donna Mobus, radio announcer on KSIR-AM, reported, "The whole ninth hole of the golf course is under water. . . . Propane tanks and those green garbage dumpsters are just being tossed around. . . . Logs, trees . . . and the speed is incredible." The flood pushed a car full of mud right into the town library.

Muddy floodwaters surge through downtown Estes Park. PHOTOGRAPH BY ROBERT D. JARRET, COURTESY OF THE U.S. GEOLOGICAL SURVEY.

As the waters receded, they left up to three feet of mud behind. Snowplows and bulldozers scraped mud and debris off the streets, and the National Guard was called in to assist Estes Park police and to prevent looting. Total damages were estimated to be $31 million, most of which was not covered by insurance.

This was the busy summer season, and many merchants were eager to clean up the mess and open their shops. Some mopped up through the night. Others looked at the mess and gave up. According to the Estes

Park *Trail Gazette*, 62 percent of the businesses on Elkhorn Avenue never reopened after the flood.

Four days after the flood, searchers found Steven See's body buried by debris. The bodies of Terry Coates and Bridget Dorris were also recovered, several miles downstream from Aspenglen Campground.

Investigators soon discovered that a leak around the three-foot-diameter outlet pipe buried in Lawn Lake Dam was at the root of the disaster. The leak had eaten away the dirt around the pipe until a trickle turned into a torrent. Rosemary Coates sued the federal government over the death of her husband, claiming that the National Park Service was negligent in monitoring the safety of dams within the park and that it also lacked warning and evacuation plans. The suit also alleged that the evacuation warning at the campground was insufficient. The court agreed and awarded Coates and her children $480,000. In the wake of the Big Thompson and Lawn Lake floods, Rocky Mountain National Park officials obtained titles to all reservoirs inside the park, removed the dams, and returned those high-country lakes to their natural sizes. The earthen embankment at Lawn Lake was removed; today, the old, higher shoreline is still visible above the lake's natural water level.

Aspenglen Campground was rebuilt, but just upstream; the only reminder of Cascade Dam is a broken concrete rampart. On the twentieth anniversary of the flood, the Estes Park Historical Society reopened the Fall River hydroelectric plant as a historical site and museum. Estes Park renovated its commercial district, adding new buildings, walkways, and green space. It's again a vibrant shopping and dining gateway to the park.

In the years following the flood, the alluvial fan at the mouth of the Roaring River became a popular tourist attraction. The park service built an interpretive path and footbridge there. In September 2013, a second flood hit the area, this time not due to a dam collapse but because of heavy rains. Both the hiking trail and footbridge were wiped out. With funding from the federal government and the Rocky Mountain Conservancy, the park's nonprofit partner, crews rebuilt the fully accessible trail and fifty-six-foot bridge so all park visitors can once again wonder at the flood's power and nature's resilience.

FRONT RANGE FLOOD, 2013

The first week of September 2013 was unusually hot in Boulder, with temperatures above 90 degrees and at least one record high. The forecast for Monday, September 9, promised relief in the form of a cold front. When the cooler air and clouds arrived, however, they stalled over the Front Range. Monday's showers turned into an inch of rain on Tuesday, followed by nearly two inches of rain on Wednesday. The ground was becoming saturated, and water was starting to pool on roadways and in low-lying areas. Then, on Thursday morning, September 12, the National Weather Service issued a warning that read in part, "Major flooding/flash flooding event underway at this time with biblical rainfall amounts reported in many areas/near the foothills—things are not looking good." Indeed, the skies had opened up, and 9.08 inches of rain fell on the Boulder area in one day.

To put that into perspective, the previous single-day rainfall record for the area was 4.8 inches, set in 1919. In fact, this new one-day record was just half an inch shy of the previous total rainfall for an entire *month*, 9.59 inches, set in May 1995. Things quickly went from "not looking good" to disastrous.

After the weekend heat wave, temperatures plummeted thirty degrees. Persistent, heavy rain poured from the sky. Soon, nearly every road heading into the foothills of Boulder, Larimer, and northern Jefferson Counties was blocked by floodwater or debris. The towns of Loveland and Longmont were basically cut in two by the Big Thompson and St. Vrain Rivers. Lyons, Estes Park, and Jamestown were completely cut off by floodwaters, and Lyons was without power. In Estes Park, telephone lines and cellphone towers were down, so ham radio operators provided emergency communications.

As the heavy rains continued, Governor John Hickenlooper declared a disaster in fourteen counties: Adams, Arapahoe, Boulder, Broomfield, Denver, El Paso, Fremont, Jefferson, Larimer, Logan, Morgan, Pueblo, Washington, and Weld. Massive runoff, mudslides, and flooding covered a 200-mile stretch of the Front Range, north to south. Several earthen dams burst or were overtopped, and numerous bridges collapsed. Raging rivers cut huge chunks out of their banks and piled enormous mounds of sediment and debris in unlikely places, cutting off roads and inundating farm fields and residential neighborhoods alike.

The heaviest rains stalled over Boulder County, and communities there were hardest hit. Boulder Creek, which normally flows at about 200 cubic feet per second (cfs) in September, was swollen to 5,000 cfs. The University of Colorado canceled classes and evacuated more than 500 students and faculty. Its website warned, "Wall of water coming down Boulder Canyon. STAY AWAY FROM BOULDER CREEK." But people gathered on bridges anyway, mesmerized by the rushing, muddy torrent. Flooding damaged at least one-quarter of the buildings on campus.

Boulder Creek churns beneath the 7th Street Bridge on September 13, 2013. PHOTOGRAPH BY KIT FULLER, COURTESY OF THE U.S. GEOLOGICAL SURVEY.

During the worst of the flood on Thursday, Wiyanna Nelson and Wesley Quinlan, both nineteen and graduates of Centaurus High School in Lafayette, Colorado, were driving home down Linden Drive from a birthday party in the mountains. Two friends, Nathan Jennings and Emily Briggs, were also in the car. At about 11 P.M., as they entered the outskirts of Boulder, their Subaru got mired in surging mud and water on the road. Quinlan urged everyone to get out of the car and wade to safety. Nelson, a former high school swimmer and water-polo player, stepped out and instantly disappeared in the torrent. Quinlan heroically jumped in to go after her. Jennings also left the car to go for help, leaving Briggs alone in the car. Briggs remembered seeing Quinlan briefly raise Nelson above the water before the current swept them both away. Jennings somehow survived, as did Briggs.

In Jamestown, a town of fewer than 300 residents about six air miles northwest of Boulder, Little James Creek had become a raging river five times its normal width. It tore houses from their foundations and scoured the roadbed from beneath James Canyon Drive, the only route in and out. Twenty percent of the houses in Jamestown were lost to floodwaters. Longtime resident Joey Howlett, seventy-two, had owned and operated the Mercantile Café ("The Merc"), serving up food, live music, and a welcoming sense of community, since 1986. Known as "the ambassador of Jamestown," Howlett was asleep in his bed at 11:30 P.M. when a debris flow careened down a gulch and buried the back of his home under twelve feet of rock

Flooding chewed through the roadbed on Lefthand Canyon Drive below Jamestown. PHOTOGRAPH BY GEOFFREY PLUMLEE, COURTESY OF THE U.S. GEOLOGICAL SURVEY.

and mud. The building collapsed, and Howlett's body was pulled from the rubble six days later.

The Boulder Valley School District also canceled classes, but that call came too late for seventy-eight fifth graders from Fireside Elementary School in Louisville, along with their teachers and adult chaperones. On Wednesday, the group had ridden buses into the mountains for three days of hiking and science activities at Cal-Wood, an environmental education facility about two miles north of Jamestown. At first, it appeared to be a typical rainy day, but by 6 P.M. the weather had deteriorated. Before long, all roads into the area were closed due to washouts. The students and adults hunkered down in the Cal-Wood Education Center. Then, on Friday, word came that they would be evacuated by helicopter. On Saturday morning, they boarded Black Hawks and Chinooks in small groups and were flown out. Including stranded residents in Jamestown and outlying homes, more than 1,200 people were airlifted to safety that day.

As bad as conditions were in the mountains, the foothills and plains weren't much better. In Broomfield, next to the Northwest Parkway, a section of Dillon Road collapsed into Rock Creek. Several motorists drove right off the broken roadway into the swollen, churning creek. Some cars flipped upside down, but rescuers arrived in time and pulled the bewildered people out of the water.

East of the mountains, flooding swamped fields and roads. PHOTOGRAPH BY KIT FULLER, COURTESY OF THE U.S. GEOLOGICAL SURVEY.

Meanwhile, in Lyons, evacuation notices went out to many residents at about 2:30 A.M. Heeding the warning, eighty-year-old Gerry Boland and his wife, Cheron, set out to stay with friends in Hygiene. Roads were bad; at some point Boland turned his car around, and they drove to Lyons Elementary School, where Boland had taught during part of his thirty-one-year career at Lyons schools. The school had been turned into an evacuation center, and the Bolands were among the first to arrive. Gerry made himself useful, turning on lights and helping to get things ready for evacuees. At some point, Gerry left the school, while Cheron stayed. He never returned. Sadly, his badly battered truck was later found 200 yards downstream from the Bolands' home, and his body was recovered a week later from the St. Vrain River.

Upstream, the St. Vrain buzz-sawed down its canyon, damaging U.S. Highway 38. Farther north, the Big Thompson River scoured its canyon and tore up sections of U.S. Highway 34. Two women in Cedar Cove near the mouth of Big Thompson Canyon were reported missing and presumed dead, and a neighbor reported seeing an eighty-year-old woman swept into the floodwaters, also presumed dead. Estes Park was effectively cut off from the outside world, and more than 1,000 residents across Larimer County were trapped when gravel mountain roads washed out. Periods of rain and fog grounded rescue helicopters, but crews sprang into action whenever weather windows allowed. They airlifted hundreds of people from outlying areas and took them to evacuation shelters.

Floodwaters collected in the South Platte River and surged out onto the plains, damaging roads and 122 bridges in Weld County alone. Neighborhoods in Greeley were submerged. Flooding destroyed or badly damaged more than 200 mobile homes and 60 houses in Evans, displacing 2,500 people. One resident, Olga Salazar, said her house flooded in thirty minutes, and she found herself in chest-deep water. Her daughter and grandson came to her rescue.

As the South Platte roiled, the towns of Goodrich, Orchard, and Weldona were told to evacuate. Near Hillrose, workers with the Burlington Northern–Santa Fe Railway quickly dumped loads of gravel for reinforcement as the South Platte River widened to within six feet of the rail bed.

Even as floodwaters receded in the coming days, standing water damaged fall crops along a wide swath of the South Platte's floodplain.

At Sterling, the South Platte was running at 23,700 cfs, fifty times its usual flow for that time of year. Water was flowing over bridges, and residents packed sandbags to protect their homes. More than 150 people were evacuated from low-lying areas between Atwood and Sterling.

The worst flooding was centered around Boulder and northern parts of the Front Range, but the rains didn't spare areas farther south. Some lower-elevation neighborhoods in Denver flooded, and metro-area rescuers used rafts to reach people stranded in cars or swamped homes.

South of Boulder, residents in Coal Creek Canyon had felt the effects of the flood as early as September 11. A flash flood poured water into the Kwik Mart store on Colorado Highway 72. An employee, Darrell Smith, said, "It was all coming down that road like a river. When they say flash flood, I always say, 'Okay, yeah, you know, you have a little water here and there,' but this got my attention." Water also inundated the building that housed the printing presses for the local newspaper. Other businesses met the same fate, and the Coal Creek flood demolished 14 homes and damaged 200 more.

On the south end of Colorado Springs, nineteen inches of rain fell on Fort Carson. A flash flood hit Sand Creek, and on September 16, police were called to East Platte Avenue about a body in the creek. The victim was identified as James Nelson Bettner, forty-seven, and the coroner gave the cause of death as accidental drowning. Bettner had given his last known address as 14 West Bijou Street, the site of the Catholic Charities Marian House and Hanifen Center, which provides services for the homeless and other people in need. He may have been bivouacked along the creek when the flood hit.

Even years after the 2013 floods, rebuilding and restoration continues. Temporary road closures and repairs have dragged on, causing frustration for locals and lost revenue from tourist trade. Two years after the flooding, the major access road to Glen Haven was still under construction, and business in the Glen Haven General Store had dropped 40 percent. Some residents in Lyons were still awaiting approval of engineering plans to rebuild their homes. In September 2020, Big Elk Meadows, a mountain community outside of Lyons, held a celebration with Boulder and Larimer county commissioners, commemorating completion of $10 million in restoration projects. These included completion of the Rainbow Lake Crossing Bridge, Sunset Lake Dam and Meadow Lake Dam, and the repair of a building for the Home Owners Association office. In July 2021—nearly eight years after the flood—officials finally announced completion of a $31 million project to rebuild and improve Colorado Highway 119 along Boulder Creek between Nederland and Boulder.

In all, the flooding destroyed more than 2,000 homes and damaged 26,000 more. Also, 200 businesses were demolished and 750 damaged. Many miles of roadways and railroad lines were submerged and damaged. At least eight people died, and two more who went missing were never found.

To date, across the fourteen counties most affected by the 2013 floods, the total cost of recovery, replacement, and rebuilding stands at more than $3 billion. Worryingly, many homes, businesses, roads, bridges, and other infrastructure still remain in flood-prone areas along the Front Range. Many people who lived through the 2013 floods will keep a wary eye on the skies whenever the forecast calls for heavy rains.

SOURCES

Great Fire and Flood in Denver, 1863-1864

"Denver's first deadly flood struck 150 years ago." Colorado Public Radio, May 16, 2014.

Grace, Stephen. *It Happened in Denver.* Two Dot Press, Globe Pequot, 2008.

"The Great Flood in Denver," *Daily Mining Journal,* May 23, 1864.

"Lessons from Denver's Flood of 1864," *Denver Post,* October 10, 2013.

"The Night Denver Burned: The Great Fire of 1863." Denver Firefighters Museum blog, August 23, 2018.

Scripps Media. "How a fire that decimated downtown Denver in the 1800s led to the city's 'brick ordinance.'" ABC 7 Denver, March 8, 2018.

Great Pueblo Flood, 1921

Blanchard, Taylor. "The D Street Operators: The women who saved thousands in Pueblo's 1921 flood." *PULP*, March 20, 2020.

Cohen, Jonathan A. "A Social and Cultural History of the Great Pueblo Flood of 1921, Its Aftermath, and Its Legacy." Master's thesis, Harvard Extension School, May 2020.

Ebersole, Samuel. "The Great Pueblo Flood, 100 Years Later." Rocky Mountain Public Broadcasting System, June 4, 2021.

Follansbee, Robert, and Edward E. Jones. "The Arkansas River Flood of June 3–5, 1921." U.S. Geological Survey Water Supply Paper 487, 1922.

Meyer, Jeremy P. "Pueblo Storm Tide Leaves Scars." *Denver Post*, March 10, 2007.

National Centers for Environmental Information. "The Month in Climate History: June 3, 1921 Colorado Flooding." National Oceanic and Atmospheric Administration, no date.

Rogers, James. "Anniversary of the Great Pueblo Flood of 1921." Denver Public Library, June 1, 2021.

Sullivan, Caitlin, Alex O'Brien, and Natalie Chuck. "100 Years Ago: The Pueblo Flood of 1921." KOAA News 5, Southern Colorado, June 2, 2021.

Denver Flood, 1965

Colorado Legislative Council, Committee on Disasters. *1965 Flood Disasters in Colorado, Report to the Colorado General Assembly.* Research Publication No. 106, November 1965.

Heberton, Brendan. "50th Anniversary of 1965 Denver Flood." *Weather5280*, June 15, 2015.

Massengill, Pat. "The 1965 Flood of the South Platte River." *My Littleton*, last modified April 2021.

Matthai, H. F. "Floods of June 1965 in South Platte River Basin, Colorado." U.S. Geological Survey Water Supply Paper 1850-B, U.S. Government Printing Office, no date.

Mayer, Kiersten J. "Gone in a flash: Castle Rock reflects on anniversary of 1965 flood." *Colorado Community Media*, June 17, 2005.

Prendergast, Alan. "The 1965 Flood: How Denver's Greatest Disaster Changed the City." *Westword*, April 29, 2015.

Prendergast, Alan. "South Platte Flood of 1965." *Colorado Encyclopedia*, last modified September 4, 2021.

Big Thompson Flood, 1976

Anderson, Barbara. *Reflections of the Heart: The Big Thompson Canyon Flood of July 31, 1976.* Drake Club Press, 1996.

Cotton, Don, ed., *The Big Thompson Flood.* C. F. Boone, 1976.

Jarrett, Robert D., and John E. Costa. "1976 Big Thompson Flood, Colorado—Thirty Years Later." Fact Sheet 2006–3095. U.S. Geological Survey, July 2006.

McComb, David. *Big Thompson: Profile of a Natural Disaster.* Pruett Publishing Co., 1980.

McKee, Spencer. "Remembering the Big Thompson flood, Colorado's deadliest natural disaster." *OutThere Colorado,* July 2, 2021.

Perry, Phyllis J. *It Happened in Rocky Mountain National Park.* Globe Pequot, 2018.

Peters, Mike. "Greeley man recalls horrible night when he lost his family in the Big Thompson Flood." *Greeley Tribune,* July 27, 2006.

Pohl, Jason. "40 years later: Scores killed in Big Thompson flood." Scottsbluff *Star-Herald,* August 7, 2016.

Sallinger, Marc. "43 years after Big Thompson flood, Flight For Life benefits from lessons learned." KUSA News 9 Denver, August 3, 2019.

Stein, Theo. "A deadly flood that helped improve weather forecasting." National Oceanic and Atmospheric Administration, July 29, 2016.

Vendegna, Michelle. "Community gathers to remember 1976 Big Thompson flood." Loveland *Reporter-Herald,* August 1, 2017.

Lawn Lake Dam Failure, 1982

Associated Press. "Hilbert man's body found." *Oshkosh Northwestern,* July 19, 1982.

Baker, Mark E. "Case Study: Lawn Lake Dam (Colorado, 1982)." Association of State Dam Safety Officials, Lessons Learned.

Baker, Mark, and Bill McCormick. *30th Anniversary of the Lawn Lake Dam Failure: A Look Back at the State and Federal Response,* Association of State Dam Safety Officials, Annual Conference, Denver, CO, July 27, 2012.

Coates v. United States, 612 F. Supp. 592. U.S. District Court for the Central District of Illinois, May 6, 1985.

Cordsen, John. "1982 flood changed face of downtown Estes Park." Estes Park *Trail Gazette,* July 12, 2012.

Darling, Dale A. *High Waters: Colorado's 2013 Flood.* River Fork Press, 2014.

Meissner, John. "1976, 1982 floods wreaked havoc on Estes Park." Estes Park *Trail Gazette,* February 24, 2021.

Miller, Gardner. *Dam! Flood!* VIP Printing, 1982.

Perry, Phyllis J. *It Happened in Rocky Mountain National Park.* Globe Pequot, 2018.

Root, Chris. "The Lawn Lake Flood." Research News, Denver Public Library, October 24, 2018.

United Press International. "Camper's body found after dam's collapse." *The New York Times,* July 17, 1982.

Front Range Flood, 2013

Aguilar, John. "'We're about to wake up': Victims of Colorado's 2013 flood look to end of recovery." *Denver Post*, September 9, 2018.

Aguilar, John, and Charlie Brennan. "Eight days, 1,000-year flood, 100-year flood." Boulder *Daily Camera*, September 21, 2013.

Brennan, Charlie. "With grit and gratitude, Jamestown rebounds 5 years after flood." Boulder *Daily Camera*, September 2, 2018.

Bryen, Whitney. "Lyons celebrates strength, though 'progress can look bleak.'" Boulder *Daily Camera*, August 28, 2014.

"Businesses Struggle to Reopen in Flood-Ravaged Coal Creek Canyon." CBS News 4 Denver, September 20, 2013.

Byars, Mitchell. "Flooding claims at least 2 lives in Boulder, Jamestown." Boulder *Daily Camera*, September 12, 2013.

City of Aurora, September 2013 Flood, Initial Report, November 11, 2013.

"CO 119 project complete today in Boulder Canyon." Colorado Department of Transportation, July 9, 2021.

"Flood Story: The 2013 Boulder, Colorado Flood." Water Damage Defense, no date.

Frosch, Dan, and Timothy Williams. "Colorado Towns are Left Stranded in Deadly Floods." *The New York Times*, September 12, 2013.

Jacobson, Willis. "Former Lompoc High athlete dies in Colorado flooding." *Santa Maria Times*, September 14, 2013.

"September 9–18, 2013 Floods." National Oceanic and Atmospheric Administration, National Weather Service, no date.

Steffen, Jordan, and Kieran Nicholson. "Colorado Flood: Front Range floodwaters kill three, drench homes." *Denver Post*, September 11, 2013.

CHAPTER 2

MASSACRES

THE COLORADO GOLD RUSH AND A LATER COAL BOOM DREW WAVES of people from a variety of cultures to the region, all looking for a better life. Sometimes these newcomers fought among themselves, usually over land, water, or other resources. More often, they clashed with the people who were already here: the Apache, Arapaho, Cheyenne, Shoshone, and Ute. The two conflicts described in this chapter have been etched into our national memory for their wanton violence and slaughter of innocents. For any compassionate person, these are difficult stories to read. But they serve as reminders of how quickly society can unravel, and they offer important lessons to prevent us from spiraling into similar tragedies again.

SAND CREEK MASSACRE, 1864

Under the terms of the Fort Laramie Treaty of 1851, the Cheyenne and Arapaho tribes were guaranteed ownership of the land between the Arkansas and North Platte Rivers. But over the next ten years, hundreds of gold prospectors and homesteaders rushed into the area. Tensions heightened between these new arrivals and the tribes, who naturally wanted whites to honor the treaty terms. On February 8, 1861, a new pact called the Treaty of Fort Wise was drawn up between the federal government and leaders of the Cheyenne and Arapaho people. The tribes ceded their rights to a vast area of the Great Plains in exchange for a 600-square-mile reservation and annuity payments. The tribal delegation included Cheyenne Chief Black Kettle and several Arapaho leaders, but they did not represent all of the tribes involved, and the new treaty was not accepted by many tribal members.

In the years that followed, fighting often broke out between whites and the tribes. Arapaho and Cheyenne raided ranches, stagecoaches, and supply lines near Denver. In May 1862, John Evans became governor of the Colorado Territory, and in November that year Colonel John Chivington took command of the U.S. Army Colorado District. These two men would play key roles in escalating conflict with the tribes.

In 1862, Chivington had played an inadvertent but pivotal role in the Battle of Glorieta Pass. That spring, Confederate troops under the command of General Henry Hopkins Sibley moved through New Mexico in an attempt to capture Fort Union, northeast of Santa Fe. But Union troops under Colonel John Slough met them at Glorieta Pass. Slough sent Chivington and his men on a flanking maneuver, but Chivington missed the main force and stumbled instead upon the enemy's supply train. He burned it, killing all the horses and mules. Although Sibley won the Battle of Glorieta Pass, the loss of all his supplies forced him to retreat to Texas and ended any Confederate plans to control the Southwest.

Chivington's slaughter of Sibley's horses and mules foreshadowed his treatment of American Indians. A now infamous quote attributed to Chivington chillingly sums up his attitude: "Damn any man who sympathizes with Indians! . . . I have come to kill Indians, and believe it is right and honorable to use any means under God's heaven to kill Indians. . . . Kill and scalp all, big and little; nits make lice."

Nor was he alone in this opinion. The *Rocky Mountain News* at the time published an opinion saying, "The tribes by which we are surrounded are our inferiors physically, morally, mentally." In the spring of 1864, U.S. Army Volunteers launched four unprovoked attacks on Cheyenne villages in the territory, sparking what was called the Indian War of 1864. In turn, warriors attacked trains, stagecoaches, and local

Colonel John Chivington's utter contempt for American Indians was central to his actions at Sand Creek. PHOTOGRAPH COURTESY OF THE DENVER PUBLIC LIBRARY, SPECIAL COLLECTIONS, Z-128.

farmsteads. In mid-May, the 1st Regiment of Colorado Volunteers attacked a Cheyenne encampment in Kansas and killed Chief Lean Bear. A month later, a white family, the Hungates, was found killed and mutilated near Denver. Despite a lack of evidence, many citizens blamed the Indians and responded with fear and anger, calling for an all-out war against the Cheyenne and Arapaho.

At the end of June 1864, Governor Evans appeared to extend an olive branch, inviting all "Friendly Indians of the Plains" to camp near military forts, where they would be given both protection and provisions. But on August 11, Evans organized the 3rd Regiment of Colorado Volunteers to "pursue, kill and destroy all hostile Indians that infest the Plains." That same day, he issued a proclamation authorizing citizens to "kill and destroy, as enemies of the country, wherever they may be found . . . hostile Indians."

In September, hoping to broker peace with the tribes, the commanding officer at Fort Lyon, Major Edward "Ned" Wynkoop, sought out Cheyenne Chief Black Kettle and other tribal leaders. They regarded Wynkoop as friendly and fair, and they agreed to go with him to Camp Weld near Denver to meet with Governor Evans. There, on September 28, Evans

At the Camp Weld council, Major Ned Wynkoop and Captain Silas Soule, kneeling in front, met with Arapaho and Cheyenne leaders, including (seated, left to right) White Antelope, Bull Bear, Black Kettle, Neva, and Na-ta-nee. PHOTOGRAPH COURTESY OF THE DENVER PUBLIC LIBRARY, SPECIAL COLLECTIONS, X-32079

warned the chiefs that their only path to peace was to surrender to Major Wynkoop at Fort Lyon. If they did so, Evans promised, the army would ensure their safety and would provide food. The chiefs warily agreed and led their people to the fort.

In November, Major Scott Anthony arrived at Fort Lyon to relieve Wynkoop of his command. The two officers met with about sixty Cheyenne and Arapaho chiefs and leaders. They told the Cheyenne to return to their camp on Sand Creek and sent the Arapaho, under Little Raven, sixty miles down the Arkansas River to wait until Major Anthony received further orders. Anthony claimed that the army could not afford to feed the tribes and that they would be better off hunting for themselves. He also promised that the U.S. Army would protect them at the designated encampments.

Meanwhile, urged on by the citizens of Denver and with the tacit support of the territorial governor, Colonel Chivington and his largely untrained and undisciplined volunteer force of 675 men headed to Fort Lyon. Learning that the Cheyenne and Arapaho had left the fort and gone to Sand Creek, Chivington placed guards around Fort Lyon to prevent anyone from leaving to warn the Cheyenne and Arapaho at Sand Creek of an impending attack. By then, as many as 750 Cheyenne and Arapaho were camped at Sand Creek, where they had been told to go.

On November 26, Major Wynkoop left Fort Lyon and traveled to his new post at Fort Riley, Kansas. On the evening of November 28, Chivington and his Colorado Volunteers left Fort Lyon and headed to the Cheyenne and Arapaho camp. They arrived at Sand Creek before daybreak on November 29, and Chivington addressed his troops as they looked down at the sleeping village of Cheyenne and Arapaho. "I don't tell you to kill all ages and sex," he said, "but look back on the Plains of the Platte, where your mothers, fathers, brothers, have been slain, and their blood saturating the sands of the Platte."

While most of the braves were out hunting for food, the Sand Creek encampment of a few Cheyenne and Arapaho warriors, along with many elderly, women, and children, was just beginning to awaken. The quiet daybreak was shattered as hundreds of U.S. soldiers suddenly appeared on the hillside and began firing cannons and rifles into the peaceful village.

White Antelope, an elderly chief of the Cheyenne, ran toward the soldiers, yelling at them not to fire. He finally stopped and folded his arms across his chest, indicating that he had no desire to fight. The soldiers fired and killed White Antelope where he stood and then rode into camp.

A few warriors escaped on horses. Black Kettle raised the American flag to show his allegiance to the U.S. government. He also put up a white flag of surrender. He called out to the approaching soldiers that this was a friendly camp, and he urged his own people not to be afraid.

Cannons fired grapeshot at tents and people. Soldiers rode through the village with sabers, killing and mutilating as they went. The Cheyenne and Arapaho were armed only with bows and arrows and clubs; they had no guns. The killing went on for eight hours. While eight of Chivington's troops were killed during the battle, somewhere between 150 and 500 Cheyenne and Arapaho were killed; more than half were women and children. The number of people killed varies in different accounts, but it is known that Colorado Volunteers went through camp killing the wounded, mutilating the dead, pillaging, and setting fire to the village.

Somehow a few Cheyenne and Arapaho managed to survive the massacre and escape the site with aid from braves returning on horseback. Among the survivors were Black Kettle, uninjured; his wife, who had been shot nine times; and the wounded Arapaho Chief Left Hand, who soon died of his wounds at a camp in the Smoky Hill area, where the survivors took refuge.

A few of Chivington's soldiers had refused to attack, including Captain Silas Soule. He said, "It looked too hard for me to see little children on their knees begging for their lives, have their brains beat out like dogs." Soule kept his squad together but did not order them to fire. Lieutenant Joseph Cramer also ignored orders to fire on the camp.

The immediate reaction of many citizens of Denver on hearing of the massacre at Sand Creek was favorable. At first, the actions of the volunteer soldiers were praised. The *Rocky Mountain News* said that the Colorado soldiers had once again "covered themselves with glory." In Denver, a holiday was declared and hundreds lined the streets as Chivington and his men paraded through town. Their display of scalps from some of the victims brought cheers from the crowd.

As more details of what actually occurred at Sand Creek came out, Congress ordered a series of investigations. Captain Soule and Lieutenant Cramer both sent letters to Major Wynkoop describing the attack. Wynkoop made copies of the letters and sent them to other army commanders and powerful politicians. Soule was one of many who later testified against Chivington. He told a friend that, by testifying, he feared that he had put his life in danger and that his character would be smeared after his death. Sadly, his concern was well founded. Eighty days after testifying on April 23, 1865, Soule was shot to death on a Denver street by a soldier named Squier, who fled to New Mexico. Squier was returned to Denver by Lieutenant Cannon of the New Mexico Volunteers. Then Cannon was found dead in his hotel room from a dose of poison, and Squier escaped.

After examining hundreds of pages of testimony, Congress said Chivington had disgraced his office and his country "by leading a foul and dastardly massacre." It ordered a court-martial. While the army investigated the incident, Denver was under martial law.

Major Edward "Ned" Wynkoop, shown here in 1861, earned Arapaho and Cheyenne leaders' trust despite their mistreatment by the U.S. Army. PHOTOGRAPH COURTESY OF THE DENVER PUBLIC LIBRARY, SPECIAL COLLECTIONS, X-22195.

Captain Silas Soule, appalled by the attack on the Sand Creek encampment, testified against Colonel Chivington. PHOTOGRAPH COURTESY OF THE DENVER PUBLIC LIBRARY, SPECIAL COLLECTIONS, X-22202.

Wynkoop was reinstated as commander of Fort Lyon, and he also investigated the incident, taking testimony from those who had been present during the attack at Sand Creek. He forwarded all of his materials to Congress, reinforcing its assessment of the atrocities that had been committed. These findings finally forced Chivington to resign his military commission and put an end to his political ambitions, but he was never punished by the army or by Congress.

Shortly after the Sand Creek Massacre, some Cheyenne warriors joined the Dog Soldiers, a group devoted to fighting the United States. They conducted raids in the Denver area on stagecoaches and wagons, partially cutting off communications with the rest of the country. Relations continued to worsen between whites and the tribes. Territorial Governor John Evans was asked by President Andrew Johnson for his resignation the following year.

Many historians cite the massacre at Sand Creek as a major cause of the twenty-five-year war between the U.S. Army and the Northern and Southern Cheyenne, Northern Arapaho, and Sioux. Just a little over a month after Sand Creek, the tribal retribution began. On January 7, 1865, 1,000 warriors—Cheyenne, Northern Arapaho, and Sioux—attacked Julesburg on the South Platte near the Colorado-Nebraska line. They killed about fifteen soldiers and looted stores. Three weeks later, war parties ranged up and down the South Platte River, capturing wagons and destroying telegraph lines. They attacked Julesburg a second time. This sort of activity continued for the next twenty-five years across Montana, South Dakota, Wyoming, Nebraska, Kansas, Oklahoma, and into Texas. In the first year of this war alone, the U.S. government spent $20 million to fight the Plains tribes.

A Civil War monument of a Union soldier was erected at the west entrance to the Capitol in Denver on July 24, 1909. At the base of the statue were tablets listing the names of battles, including Sand Creek, and those killed in each. No one had questioned this at the time the statue was erected, but in the 1990s some people objected, saying Sand Creek was more of a massacre than a battle. A controversy arose. It was decided to leave the statue and tablet in place but to add a fifth plaque. It states, "By designating Sand Creek a battle, the monument's designers mischaracterized the actual events. Protests led by some Sand Creek descendants and others through-out the twentieth century have led to the widespread recognition of the tragedy of the Sand Creek Massacre."

In 1998, U.S. Senator Ben Nighthorse Campbell sponsored legislation to memorialize the Sand Creek Massacre site. But historians, archaeologists, and the tribes could not agree on the site's exact location. In part, this was because Chivington's attack expanded beyond the encampment as the victims fled. Researchers pored over historical accounts and aerial photo-graphs, and tribal members compared oral histories with on-the-ground landmarks. Experts with metal detectors searched key points along Sand Creek, eventually finding clusters of spent rifle cartridges and various tools and utensils. An archivist sorting records in the National Archives–Great Lakes Region in Chicago found an 1868 map of the massacre site drawn by U.S. Army Lieutenant Samuel Bonsall. Considering all of this evidence, all parties finally agreed that the key events occurred within an area 5.5 miles long and 2 miles wide along Sand Creek east-northeast of Eads, Colorado. In 2000, Congress established Sand Creek as an official historic site to recognize the significance of the massacre in American history, and its ongoing significance to the Arapaho and Cheyenne people and the descen-dants of the massacre victims. In 2005, President George W. Bush gave final approval, and Sand Creek Massacre Historical Site opened to the public in 2007. In December 2014, John Hickenlooper became the first Colorado governor to apologize for the tragedy. "We should not be afraid to criticize and condemn that which is inexcusable," he said to a crowd gathered at the Capitol in Denver. "On behalf of the state of Colorado, I want to apologize. We will not run from this history."

LUDLOW MASSACRE, 1914

Mineral riches drove much of Colorado's early Euro-American settlement, and the state continues to rank among the top twenty mineral producers in the nation. From the 1800s onward, mines spat out gold, silver, lead, and other precious metals, as well as prodigious amounts of coal. At its peak in 1910, the coal-mining industry in Colorado produced more than 12 million tons of coal a year (by hand) and employed nearly 16,000 people, or 10 percent of the state work force. Vestiges of that era remain today in the names of communities such as Coaldale, Coal Creek, Coalmont, Cokedale, and Boncarbo.

Three companies dominated coal mining in Colorado. Chief among them was the Colorado Fuel and Iron Company (CF&I), a steel conglomerate controlled by East Coast investors George Jay Gould and John D. Rockefeller (and his son, John Jr.). The company operated twenty-three mines in Colorado, nine coking plants, and a large steel mill in Pueblo, that city's major industry for many years.

In those early years, the fatality rate of Colorado coal miners was double that of the rest of the nation. Working conditions in the mines were extremely hazardous and grim. Many miners worked twelve-hour shifts, six days a week. Explosions and cave-ins occurred often, and deadly gases were a constant worry. More than 1,700 Colorado miners died in mining accidents in the twenty-eight years between 1884 and 1912. Some mining companies, like Phelps Dodge, which ran the Stag Canyon Mine in Dawson, New Mexico, installed state-of-the-art (for the time) safety equipment (such as huge Sirocco fans for ventilation) and provided medical clinics to care for sick and injured workers. Other companies, including CF&I, paid only lip service to employee well-being.

If the job was dangerous, it was also demeaning. The men were not paid by the hour but by how many tons of coal they brought out. Nor were they paid for so-called "dead time," the hours spent placing timbers to shore up the tunnels or laying tracks for the ore cars. Miners also complained that the weigh-in man frequently tipped the scales against them when recording the amount of coal they dug. Those who raised concerns about the pitiable conditions were fired. They had no union to represent their interests.

In the mines of northern Colorado, most of the workers had been born in the United States and spoke English. In the coalfields around Trinidad in southern Colorado, however, most of the miners were immigrants from Greece, Croatia, Italy, Austria, Serbia, Germany, Romania, Bulgaria,

Hungary, Russia, and Poland. Many spoke little English, and some lacked mining experience, making them more susceptible to accidents and company duplicity.

Many of the small towns where the miners lived were little more than fenced company camps. The mine owners hired armed guards to enforce curfews and dictate who or what came into and out of the camps. In lieu of money, miners were paid in scrip, redeemable only at company stores that charged inflated prices. In short, the company mistreated its miners but demanded their complete fealty, much like a malevolent feudal lord ruling his serfs.

Given the circumstances, it's no surprise that tensions between company management and labor had been building for years. In 1894, hard-rock (gold and silver) miners in Cripple Creek went on strike when mine owners tried to increase shift length from eight to ten hours without raising pay. To break the strike, the mine owners recruited a private army of 1,200 men, deputized by the county sheriff. Miners armed themselves and prepared for the worst. But Governor Davis Waite intervened, sending in the Colorado National Guard to disband the private army, and persuaded the mine owners to return to eight-hour shifts and a wage of $3 per day.

Over the next decade, hard-rock miners across the state organized under the Western Federation of Miners (WFM), and strikes were a regular occurrence, with the eight-hour workday as the primary point of contention. In 1903, this trend culminated in the Colorado Labor Wars, which pitted hard-rock miners and other laborers against mine owners and a larger circle of business owners and employers. The "wars" lasted from May 1903 into the summer of 1904. In that time, two striking miners and seventeen strike-breakers and non-union men were killed and hundreds of union miners were illegally "deported" out of Colorado. Through a pattern of calculated violence, the Colorado National Guard affirmed its pro-business, anti-labor stance, even to the point of skirting or defying state laws, including the Colorado Constitution. This set an ominous precedent that would bear deadly fruit in Ludlow less than ten years later.

By 1900, the United Mine Workers of America (UMWA) union was organizing coal miners in the western states. Company owners did their best to tamp out any flickers of union interest. CF&I hired the Baldwin-Felts Detective Agency, which favored aggressive, often violent, strike-breaking tactics. Miners who tried to organize were fired, taken across state lines, beaten, and warned never to return. Their replacements were often foreign-born workers who accepted low wages and dire working conditions. CF&I mines continued to be deadly; in 1910 alone, coal-dust explosions in Primero and Starkville killed 131 men.

In mid-1913, mindful of the strife during the Labor Wars, Governor Elias Ammons sent representatives to Trinidad to broker an agreement between miners, union organizers, and mine owners. But in August 1913, two Baldwin-Felts men, Walter Belk and George Belcher, recently deputized by the Huerfano County sheriff, shot and killed UMWA organizer Gerald Lippiatt in downtown Trinidad. Local authorities refused to investigate the murder. Undeterred, coal miners in the Trinidad coalfields formed a local chapter that September under UMWA. With support from union and labor advocate Mother Jones, who gave a speech in Trinidad (see sidebar), they made a list of demands: recognition of a union; a pay raise; an eight-hour workday; pay for support work such as timbering and laying track; elections to designate the weigh-in man; the right to trade at stores of their choosing, select their own lodging, and choose their own doctor; elimination of armed camp guards; and enforcement of Colorado mining laws.

CF&I rejected all of the demands, so on September 23, 1913, the miners went on strike. Within a few days, more than 7,000 miners across the region joined the work stoppage. CF&I responded by evicting miners from company camps and towns. UMWA leased land and moved striking miners into tent camps at Walsenburg, Rugby, Aguilar, Forbes, Suffield, Sopris, Starkville, and, the largest camp, Ludlow.

CF&I then brought in scabs (non-union workers) and told the Baldwin-Felts men to use any means to break the strike. The Baldwin-Felts men used the CF&I shop to outfit a touring car with steel-plated armor and mount a Colt-Browning M1895 machine gun that could fire 450 rounds a minute. They drove the car, nicknamed the "Death Special," around the perimeters of striking tent camps at night, shining searchlights at the tents and firing rifles and the machine gun into them at random. Terrorized, the miners dug pits beneath their tent homes as safe havens from the bullets. In many ways, the coalfields resembled a war zone and the Death Special looked like a tank.

In response, striking miners went to Walsenburg to stock up on guns, ammunition, and explosives. With all sides armed and quarrelsome, violent confrontations occurred almost daily. Striking miners assaulted scabs, deputies and guardsmen beat strikers, and everyone took occasional pot-shots at their enemies. It didn't help ease tensions when on October 22 a coal-dust explosion at the Stag Canyon Mine in Dawson, New Mexico (just forty-five miles south of Ludlow), killed 263 men.

As the situation grew more tense, the Huerfano and Las Animas County sheriffs recruited more deputies. In late October, some of these new deputies encountered a hostile crowd of strikers while escorting wagons belonging to a scab. The deputies fired into the strikers and killed three of them.

One of the new deputies was a soldier of fortune, Karl Linderfelt, a man with a fascination for things military and a reputation for gratuitous brutality. He had served in the Colorado National Guard during the 1903

Karl Linderfelt, center, was known even among his fellow guardsmen for a penchant for brutality.
PHOTOGRAPH COURTESY OF THE SURVEY.

Colorado Labor Wars and eventually rose to the rank of second lieutenant. On October 24, 1913, he led a "militia" of twenty deputies and National Guardsmen to Ludlow to secure CF&I property. The striking miners saw this either as a threat or an opportunity, and they fired rifles at Linderfelt's unit from the flanks of nearby Berwind Canyon. Guardsman Joe Nimmo was shot and killed, and the militia pursued the strikers up the canyon to the CF&I town of Berwind. There, the strikers pinned down the militia with rifle fire until forty more guardsmen and Baldwin-Felts men arrived carting a tripod-mounted machine gun. The militia was able to retreat to safety, but this incident likely poured fuel onto Linderfelt's hostility toward the strikers.

The Berwind Canyon skirmish also stirred Governor Ammons to officially deploy the Colorado National Guard to the Trinidad coalfields on October 28 under the command of General John Chase. If Linderfelt was a loose cannon, Chase was a tyrant whose sense of law and order wasn't troubled by actual laws or legal precedents. In the December 5, 1914, issue of the *Survey* (a national magazine), reporter John Fitch described Chase as:

[A] narrow-minded man and something of an egotist. He believes intensely that he is right, and his mind once made up is difficult to change. Chase doesn't believe in strikes and has no sympathy with workingmen. . . . It was a mistake to send such a man into a strike region at the head of the state militia. But it was worse than a mistake to send Chase, for his record is well known to all the labor men in the state and his presence could only inspire suspicion and fear of the militia.

Indeed, Chase's "record" was far from impartial. It had been General Chase who placed miners (and even a county commissioner) under military arrest in Cripple Creek during the 1903 Labor Wars and then ordered his troops, with rifles loaded and bayonets fixed, to storm the courtroom during a hearing on why the men were being held. Chase's troops had also trained a Gatling gun on the courthouse. The judge, however, was not intimidated and ordered the release of the prisoners. In a mad act of hubris,

Chase faced the judge and said, "Acting under the orders of the commander-in-chief, I must at this time decline to obey the order of the court." He sent the miners back to jail, where they were held until the governor ordered them set free. Chase was court-martialed and convicted of disobedience for his actions in Cripple Creek, but the governor immediately restored him as commander of the state National Guard "in view of the general's previous good record."

So it was that General Chase was in command of 931 National Guard troops in 1913 as the Colorado Coalfield War spiraled out of control. On November 1, Chase posted his troops in two camps, one in Trinidad and one in Walsenburg. Fearing that more armed troops were coming by rail, striking miners shot at

Callous and egotistical, General John Chase, left, had a knack for escalating already combative situations. PHOTOGRAPH COURTESY OF THE DENVER PUBLIC LIBRARY, SPECIAL COLLECTIONS, X-60525.

a passing train from nearby ridgelines, with little effect. But the National Guard responded, along with a group of CF&I mine guards. One mine guard was killed, and the next day strikers set several buildings on fire in Aguilar. National Guardsmen arrested several strikers for arson.

Later that November, strikers and mine owners agreed to disarm, but National Guardsmen collected only twenty to thirty guns from the strikers' tent camps. A string of incidents over the following weeks showed that the striking miners were still angry and armed. When a non-union miner refused to join the union, strikers ambushed him and his CF&I escort, killing a driver and three guards. That same day, a strikebreaker being escorted through a crowd of union supporters was shot in the head. Then a clerk working at the McLaughlin Mine was assaulted by strikers, and a non-striker's home was dynamited. In late November, George Belcher (one of the Baldwin-Felts men accused of killing Gerald Lippiatt) was gunned down in Trinidad. The next month, strikers killed a mine guard in Delagua, northwest of Ludlow.

Mother Jones returned to Trinidad in January 1914. She was promptly arrested by order of General Chase, which sparked a protest march and garnered national headlines. In short order, the Congressional House Committee on Mines and Mining opened an investigation into the Colorado coalfield strikes.

Things were relatively quiet between the National Guardsmen and the miners in January until some guardsmen encountered barbed wire on a path and blamed it on a boy from a striking miner's family. Linderfelt went to the Ludlow colony of miners, questioned the Greek union leader Louis Tikas on the whereabouts of the boy, and when he didn't receive the information he wanted, hit Tikas in the face. Many believed that Linderfelt was trying to provoke the strikers to violence.

On March 10, 1914, when a non-striking miner's body was found by the railroad tracks near the tent city of Forbes, the National Guard accused strikers of murder. When the people from Forbes were away attending a funeral for two young children, the National Guard destroyed the tent camp.

By then, with the help of the National Guard and Baldwin-Felts, CF&I had managed to replace the strikers with non-union men in the mines, and coal production was returning to normal. In early April, hoping for the best and looking to cut expenses, Governor Ammons recalled most of the National Guard, leaving only one detachment of guardsmen, called Troop A, which was filled mostly by CF&I and Baldwin-Felts guards.

No one knows for certain what went wrong at Ludlow on the morning of April 20. A group of guardsmen led by Major Pat Hamrock had taken up positions with machine guns on high ground overlooking the camp, setting people in the camp on edge. Hamrock then requested a meeting with the camp leader, Tikas, at a train depot half a mile from camp. Tikas went, but fearing a trap, he ran back into the camp. Suddenly, three explosions rent the air. Hamrock had set them off as a signal to Linderfelt to bring his men from their camp up Berwind Canyon. Strikers and National Guardsmen all began shooting, and women and children in camp either tried to flee to a nearby arroyo or ducked into pits dug beneath their tents. When Linderfelt and his men arrived, they rampaged on horseback through camp, firing their guns. They dipped brooms in kerosene and lit them to use as torches, setting fire to as many tents as they could.

A man stands in shock amid the remains of the Ludlow camp after Linderfelt's men torched it. PHOTOGRAPH COURTESY OF THE NATIONAL ARCHIVES.

Shooting continued throughout the day, with National Guard machine guns spraying camp from Water Tank Hill. At some point, Linderfelt's men captured Tikas, and Linderfelt clubbed him with the butt of a rifle. Tikas' body was later found, shot three times in the back.

After the fighting stopped, searchers found eleven children and two women suffocated by smoke or burned to death in one of the shelter pits. A final death toll was never confirmed, but most scholars believe it was between nineteen and twenty-five people. One historian argues that as many as fifty-five, mostly women and children, died in the camp.

When the funerals for the Ludlow victims were held in Trinidad, hundreds of mourners paraded without violence. News of the events at Ludlow quickly reached Walsenburg and other striking tent colonies. Then the reprisals began. This was the beginning of the Ten Day War. Newspapers such as the *Daily Camera* and the *Rocky Mountain News*, which had previously been biased toward the mine owners, now switched their sympathies to the miners. Strikers across the region attacked scabs and company guards, and minor battles erupted at other camps, and even in Walsenburg, from day to day. The northernmost battle took place on

April 28 at the Hecla mine in Louisville. In response, General Chase called in 362 National Guardsmen who fought to regain control of the unraveling situation.

Then, in Denver, more than 1,000 members of the Women's Peace Association held a sit-in at the Capitol, persuading Governor Ammons to ask President Woodrow Wilson to send federal troops to the strike zone. Federal troops arrived in Denver on April 29 and moved immediately to Trinidad, where they were welcomed by miners. President Wilson also offered to help with negotiations, but John D. Rockefeller declined because Wilson argued for allowing the miners to engage in collective bargaining. President Wilson then pressured Governor Ammons to take decisive action. On May 2, Ammons assured Wilson that the military was leaving the area, and he issued a proclamation that "all persons not in the military service of the United States" were to disarm. With a strong presence of U.S. soldiers and state officials appearing to hold both sides accountable, the violence finally ebbed. Yet some aspects of the strike continued until December, when the union ran out of funds.

The total number of people killed in the Ludlow Massacre and the Ten Day War remains unknown. The Las Animas County coroner reported a total of 232 violent deaths; the actual number may be much higher. The Associated Press at the time pegged the financial cost at $18 million, equivalent to more than $450 million today. Many of the participants were brought to trial, but meaningful convictions were few. In May 1914, Lieutenant Linderfelt was tried in Golden in a military court. He admitted to striking Tikas with a rifle. He was found guilty of assault, but the court did not attach any criminality to his actions. He was, however, reduced in rank. More than 400 miners were accused of crimes including murder, but only four were convicted. A striker named John Lawson was found guilty of murder and sentenced to prison, but UMWA insisted he was innocent. In 1917, the Colorado Supreme Court overturned his conviction.

Rockefeller hired people to help him create a system whereby miners could have internal representation in CF&I. He even met with Mother Jones. In time, these steps evolved into the Colorado Industrial Plan and the creation of a CF&I company union.

In 1916, UMWA purchased a forty-acre lot encompassing the spot where the Ludlow tent camp had been and began work on a monument to commemorate this calamity. It was dedicated in 1918. The monument features statues of a man, woman, and child. In May 2003, vandals damaged the statues; repairs were unveiled in 2005. The Ludlow site was designated a National Historic Landmark in 2009.

The events at Ludlow and the Ten Day War remain among the bloodiest disputes between management and labor in U.S. history.

THE UNION ORGANIZER MARY HARRIS
"Mother" Jones garnered national attention for the coalfield strikers when she led a march on the town hall in Trinidad in 1913 and gave speeches inside and out. In her speech on September 25, Jones said, "When we strike, we strike to win." A federal attorney once called her "the most dangerous woman in America."

Mother Jones was one of the best-known women of her time, and she knew how to leverage her public image.

Mary Harris "Mother" Jones was a tireless advocate for workers' rights. PHOTOGRAPH COURTESY OF THE LIBRARY OF CONGRESS, LC-USX62-50377.

She was born in Cork, Ireland, in 1837 and as a child moved with her family to Toronto, Canada, to escape the potato famine. She became a dressmaker and a schoolteacher. Harris taught at schools in Michigan and Chicago and eventually landed in Memphis, Tennessee, where she married George Jones, a foundry worker and member of the International Iron Molders Union. Mary and George had four children. Then, in 1867, a yellow-fever epidemic killed George and all four children. Mary returned to Chicago and worked as a dressmaker until her shop and home were destroyed in the Great Chicago Fire of 1871. She then worked to help rebuild Chicago. She joined the Knights of Labor and was soon organizing strikes. By 1897, Jones was an

effective and popular public speaker advocating for working men and women. She wore vintage black dresses and roamed America, with no permanent address. She spoke in support of government workers in Chicago, bottle washers in Milwaukee, and steelworkers in Pittsburgh. Although she was sometimes jailed and didn't win every battle, Mother Jones made a difference. Even when white-haired and seventy-six years old, her presence in the Colorado coalfields sent a message that was heard across the country.

SOURCES

Sand Creek Massacre, 1864

"A timeline of events relating to the Sand Creek Massacre." Sand Creek Massacre National Historic Site, National Park Service, last modified March 17, 2019.

"Nov. 29, 1864: Sand Creek Massacre." This Day in History. Zinn Education Project. www.zinnedproject.org/news/tdih/sand-creek-colo-massacre.

Coel, Margaret. *Chief Left Hand.* University of Oklahoma Press, 1981.

Grace, Stephen. *It Happened in Denver.* TwoDot, Globe Pequot Press, 2007.

Hernandez, Elizabeth. "Gov. Hickenlooper apologizes to descendants of Sand Creek Massacre." *Denver Post,* December 3, 2014.

Hoig, Stan. *The Sand Creek Massacre.* University of Oklahoma Press, 2013.

Perry, Phyllis J. *Speaking Ill of the Dead: Jerks in Colorado History.* Globe Pequot Press, 2011.

Roberts, Gary L. *Massacre at Sand Creek.* Abingdon Press, 2016.

Ludlow Massacre, 1914

"Berwind, Colorado." Wikiwand, accessed November 12, 2021.

"Chase Court-Martial: Objections of Defendant Were All Overruled." *Deseret News,* October 20, 1903.

"Chase's Record Saves Him: Court-Martial Findings Approved, but Governor Restores General to Duty." *The New York Times,* November 8, 1903.

DeMaio, Dennis. "Memorial Desecrated." *People's World,* June 12, 2003.

Dobson, G. B. "The Ludlow Massacre." Wyoming Tales and Trails, no date.

Fitch, John A. "Law and Order: The Issue in Colorado." *The Survey,* December 5, 1914.

Johnson, Marilynn S. *Violence in the West.* St. Martins, 2009.

Larsen, Natalie. "Conditions at the CFI Mines of the Colorado Coalfields." *Intermountain Histories*, accessed November 19, 2021.

Laughlin, Rosemary. *The Ludlow Massacre of 1912–14*. Morgan Reynolds Publishing, 2006.

Martelle, Scott. *Blood Passion: The Ludlow Massacre and Class War of the American West*. Rutgers University Press, 2007.

Perry, Phyllis J. *Speaking Ill of the Dead: Jerks in Colorado History*. Globe Pequot Press, 2011.

Rees, Jonathan H. "Colorado Fuel and Iron." *Colorado Encyclopedia*, last modified January 31, 2021.

Sampson, Joanna. *Remember Ludlow*. Colorado Historical Society, 1999.

CHAPTER 3

TRAIN WRECKS

IN THE 1800S, RAILROADS WERE CRUCIAL TO COLORADO'S DEVELOPMENT and connection to the outside world, but getting the lines built was a challenging process. Congress passed the Pacific Railway Act in 1862, promising rail service to the growing town of Denver, but five years would pass before the first railroad came to Colorado, and that was a nine-mile extension from Nebraska to Julesberg. In frustration, Governor John Evans remarked, "Colorado without railroads is comparatively worthless."

In response, Denver business owners created the Denver Pacific Railway and Telegraph Company and completed a line from Denver to Cheyenne in 1870. Over the next twenty years, rail lines sprang up throughout the state, linking gold camps to cities and coal mines to steel mills. Along with this surge in rail routes came a wave of train accidents, including two that remain shocking for their grisly scenes and loss of life.

Today, throughout the United States, passenger rail is one of the safest ways to travel, second only to commercial airline flight. Rail accidents are rare, and most fatalities associated with rail traffic aren't passengers but pedestrians and motorists struck by trains.

TRAIN WRECK AT EDEN, 1904

In the early 1900s, passenger rail was the fastest and most comfortable way to travel between most Colorado cities. The same trains often connected to more distant destinations as well, linking the state to the rest of the country. Such was the case with the Missouri Pacific *Flyer*, which ran from St. Louis, Missouri, to Pueblo, Colorado, and then up to Denver on Denver & Rio

Grande Western Railroad tracks, with a stop at Colorado Springs. Inbound to Denver, the train was known as the No. 12. In Denver, it was cleaned, restocked, and restaffed. Then it headed back to Pueblo and points east as No. 11. The run between Denver and Pueblo took three hours and fifteen minutes, about the same amount of time needed today to drive the 115 miles on Interstate 25. In 1904, such efficiency must have felt luxurious. Residents of Pueblo often took the train to enjoy a weekend in the capital, returning on Sunday evening.

Such was the case just before 5 P.M. on August 7, 1904, as people waited at the Denver station to board the No. 11. The engine would be pulling a short tender full of coal and six cars: a baggage car, a coach car, a chair car, two Pullman sleeping cars, and a dining car. After boarding passengers, the train left Denver at 5:05 P.M. Henry Hinman was the engineer and David Mayfield was the fireman (who topped off the boiler's water tank and fed coal into the firebox). The conductor was James Smith, whose wife was also on board.

At Colorado Springs, about fifty more passengers boarded the train. Engineer Hinman received a bulletin warning of a thunderstorm headed toward Pueblo and alerting him to the possibility of flooded sections of track. Following orders, Hinman slowed the train, although he was running about fifteen minutes late. Twelve miles south of Colorado Springs, at the town of Fountain, the passengers could see through the windows that there was snow or hail on the ground, and many marveled at what appeared to be snow in August. At this point, it grew dark, and lightning flashed across the sky. No. 11 continued south at its slower pace.

Unknown to everyone on the train, a dangerous situation was developing at Hogan's Gulch, also known as Dry Creek (today's Porter Creek), twenty-two miles south of Fountain. Runoff from the thunderstorm was funneling toward the sharply incised gulch—about fifty feet wide and fifteen deep—and the creek was rising rapidly. Not long before No. 11 arrived at the gulch, a county road bridge upstream collapsed and was carried into the railway span, Bridge 110-B. Water piled up against the blockage, and the railroad bridge supports strained against the added load.

No. 11 was due in Pueblo at 8:15 P.M., but the slow-moving train was just crossing Bridge 110-B, eight miles from Eden station in Pueblo, at 8:20 P.M. At that very moment, a flash flood surged and a wave swept over the bridge. The locomotive had just reached the far side of the bridge when the wave hit the train broadside. Hinman felt the engine sway as the bridge groaned, and he gave it more throttle in an attempt to finish the crossing. But the impact of the water stopped the train and jerked it backward, snapping a coupling just in front of the two sleeping cars and dining car, breaking the train at its midsection as the bridge collapsed. The engine, tender, and three lead cars fell backward into the raging water. Luckily, when the coupling broke, the three rear cars stopped. Reports suggested that either the emergency air brakes engaged automatically or the Pullman car's porter, Melville Sales of St. Louis, quickly activated the brakes. The first Pullman car stopped with its front end dangling four feet over the gulch on the broken tracks.

People in the back half of the train did not realize at first what had happened. Several thought that, because of water on the track, the train had simply stopped. When they saw that half the train was missing, some thought the front of the train had made it across the bridge and was on the other side. It was too dark to see down into the water or across to the far side of the bridge. The passengers in the rear of the train eventually got out and built a fire, where they huddled and waited to learn what was going on. Accounts vary, but it seems that some of those passengers walked to Eden station for help through what was now very heavy rain.

One passenger who survived wrote a firsthand account that appeared in the *Pueblo Wage Earner* on August 25, 1904. "Suddenly there was a jolt as if the car had struck some solid object, and immediately another, the car shivering, and grinding and trembling, as if in fright," he wrote. "There was no noise, no cries—nothing to indicate that the most horrible railroad wreck in the history of the world had occurred; nothing to tell of the death struggle of the hundred men, women, and children who a moment before were a joyous assemblage in the cars ahead of them."

The engine, tender, and three cars had fallen from the bridge into the normally dry arroyo, which now was filled with a torrent of muddy water. The bridge itself, along with several cars and most of their occupants, was carried away. The floodwaters emptied into Fountain Creek less than a half mile from the bridge; from there, Fountain Creek runs about eight miles to join the Arkansas River. The train engine had landed on its right side and, being heavy, settled into the mud as the flood washed over it. The chair car was carried to Fountain Creek and then another half mile downstream. Other cars were later discovered more than four miles down Fountain Creek, halfway to Pueblo.

The fireman, Mayfield, reported hearing the crashing of timbers as he leapt from the engine before it was sucked back into the flood. He landed in the water and was struck by a timber. Swept downstream, he desperately clawed his way ashore, still within sight of the locomotive's headlight beaming into the night sky. He called out for engineer Hinman but got no response. Mayfield yelled to the survivors at the rear of the train and, assured that they were safe, began walking to Eden station for help.

The torrent tumbled the first three cars as they washed downstream, and the chances of survival were slim for their crew members and passengers. One passenger, John Killin, was in one of the cars hurtling down the creek. The windows smashed and water filled the car. Killin held his breath, preparing to crawl out one of the windows, but suddenly the roof of the car peeled off and he swam free. He was immediately struck by a railroad tie, which he grabbed for flotation. Killin struggled to hold onto the tie, but he eventually reached shallow water and managed to wade ashore. (Killin reportedly displayed the railroad tie at his shop in Pueblo as a memento of his brush with death.) Two other passengers, Henry Gilbert and Tony Fisher, escaped from a front car and swam to solid ground.

Word of the disaster did not reach Pueblo for several hours, but soon a rescue train headed north, carrying as many doctors as could be found, as well as the superintendent of the Pueblo Division of the Denver & Rio Grande Railroad, R. H. Bowron. At about 11 P.M., a second rescue train left Pueblo with more volunteers, police, stretchers, medical supplies, and coffins. Using lanterns and lighting fires along the riverbanks for light and heat, rescue teams searched for survivors. That first night, they found six bodies, including that of engineer Hinman. His body lay about 200 feet from the wreckage. He apparently was thrown into the floodwaters when the engine careened backward. At about 1:45 A.M., the first rescue train returned to Pueblo with those who had survived the wreck unscathed, along with others who had been injured and treated at the scene.

The next day, August 8, searchers continued looking for victims, and the power and extent of the flood was beginning to become apparent. Flotsam and bodies were scattered for miles downstream. The *Alamosa Journal* reported, "With the breaking of day the full horror of the scene, which was concealed to a great degree by the mantle of night, became apparent. Wreckage is visible in all directions, dead bodies being visible here and there in the piles of debris from the cars, driftwood and mud."

On August 9, Pueblo Mayor Benjamin B. Brown called a public meeting to organize patrols along both Fountain Creek and the Arkansas River in an attempt to locate more of the bodies of victims. The coroner happened to be out of town, but a local judge and the district attorney impaneled a six-man coroner's jury to investigate the accident. The jury was tasked with determining responsibility for the accident and whether anyone bore criminal culpability. The members of the coroner's jury promptly visited the accident site to begin their investigation.

The search for bodies continued far downstream on August 10. By then, the list of identified dead stood at seventy-one, with another three bodies unidentified and twenty-eight people still unaccounted for. It was clear, however, that the effort was no longer about rescuing survivors but recovering bodies. Fountain Creek had receded to a normal level, and up to 500 people were aiding police in the search. Bloodhounds were brought in, but they floundered in quicksand. The sheer geographic scope of the search was vast—several cars were discovered four miles downstream filled with sand, and one woman's body, "handsomely dressed," was found twenty-two miles down the Arkansas River.

The conductor's passenger list had been lost in the wreck, so no one knew exactly how many passengers and crew had been on board the train; the best estimate was about 125 people. As the body count grew, undertakers and embalmers were brought in from out of town. Most of the victims were from Pueblo, and the city went into deep mourning, with a steady stream of funerals. J. Q. Thomas, commercial agent for the Santa Fe Railroad, and his wife died in the wreck, leaving four orphans. Newspapers

Scene of the Wreck—the Locomotive, half buried in the Mud, being raised by the Wrecking Crew

A Chair-car, filled with Victims, overturned in the Stream

PHOTOGRAPHS OF THE RECENT DISASTROUS WRECK ON THE DENVER AND RIO GRANDE RAILROAD

One of the worst railroad wrecks in the history of the country occurred on August 7, near Eden, Colorado, when the "World's Fair Flyer" on the Denver and Rio Grande Railroad ran into an abyss through a bridge over Dry Creek, which had been washed away. More than eighty persons lost their lives by the accident. The engine and first three cars of the train fell into the stream below, and only a few of the occupants escaped. The passengers in two sleeping-cars which remained on the track were uninjured

1312

Top: A crane was used to lift the locomotive out of the mud in the Dry Gulch channel.
Bottom: The chair car, "filled with victims," rests submerged in floodwaters. PHOTOGRAPHS COURTESY OF THE DENVER PUBLIC LIBRARY, SPECIAL COLLECTIONS, Z-8755.

noted that the Gartland family of Denver suffered a severe loss: the mother, Kate, died, along with four of her five children. The list of victims covered a cross-section of life in Pueblo: Edward Curtis, brick mason; Miss Bennell, nurse; Alice Sturgeon, shop clerk; Alexander Maxwell, bookkeeper; H. R. Graves, plumber; John Bishop, architect; Stella McDonald, teacher at Central High School. A handful of victims were from farther afield: Utah, Kansas, Iowa, Missouri, Tennessee, Illinois, Ohio, Massachusetts, and even Jacksonville, Florida.

The coroner's jury met six times over eleven days after the wreck. They heard accounts from fifty witnesses and made six trips to the accident site. The jury determined that the Denver & Rio Grande Railroad was responsible for the wreck due to poor design and construction of Bridge 110-B. They also said the railroad lacked flagmen, track walkers, and an adequate reporting system for safety issues. The jury held that the train crew was blameless, and it refrained from suggesting that criminal charges be brought against the railroad. This outcome didn't satisfy many of the victims' families, and much of the public believed that the wreck was due to criminal negligence.

Remarkably, within twenty-four hours of the wreck, the railroad erected a new bridge, even as the locomotive still rested in the mud below. A passenger train traveled the route the very next day, even while crews tried to salvage the No. 11 locomotive. A crane brought in from Pueblo wasn't strong enough, but a bigger crane from Salida finally pulled the engine from the muck. The railroad estimated the damage to the train and track at $25,000. Another $300,000 would be needed to settle lawsuits for personal injuries and deaths. In Colorado at the time, statutes limited death settlements to $5,000 per person. Often, however, families settled for considerably less.

Almost a month after the accident, Tony Fisher, one of the few people from the front of the train who initially survived, died of a tetanus infection in his wounds. That brought the final tally of fatalities to ninety-seven. Another fourteen people, including nine-year-old Walter Gartland, were never found. The wreck of the No. 11 remains the deadliest train wreck in Colorado history and the fourth deadliest in the United States.

DOTSERO TRAIN COLLISION, 1909

Many major disasters are caused by natural events: storms, floods, lightning-caused wildfires, earthquakes, and so on. But sometimes human error—or hubris—leads to serious carnage. Also, we have a tendency to sprint ahead in using our newest technology before working out all the kinks. The education gained through trial and error can be costly—and sometimes lethal.

As a case in point, railroad operators in the mid-1800s routinely sent trains zipping down the rails without widespread agreement on departure and arrival times. Not only did this give schedulers and conductors headaches, but it greatly increased the risk of collisions. The problem centered on the long-standing convention that each town across the country would set its clocks to local time based on the sun's highest point in the sky at noon. But "noon" occurs at different times as you move east or west. For example, moving west, noon occurs four minutes later for each degree of longitude. From its border with Kansas to its border with Utah, Colorado spans seven degrees of longitude—a twenty-eight-minute difference between solar noon from one end of the state to the other. When it comes to railroad schedules, such discrepancies are the stuff of disaster.

The chief engineer of the Canadian Pacific Railway, Sandford Fleming, proposed a system of international standard time zones in 1878. Though this was heralded as an ingenious solution to the problem of local time, it was not widely adopted in the United States until the 1890s, and compliance remained spotty until Congress passed the Standard Time Act of 1918.

Complicating matters further, few rail lines had adequate signals. In 1909, only about one-fifth of the nation's rail lines were equipped with so-called block signal systems, in which traffic on sections or "blocks" of a rail line is controlled by colored lights (the signals), indicating whether the track ahead is clear or occupied. Instead, train engineers relied on time-tables and their pocket watches (and in some places, telegraphs between stations) to determine whether it was safe to proceed. Often, this meant waiting on a siding—a stretch of track parallel to the main line—until an oncoming train passed. If the oncoming train was delayed, the waiting engineer had almost no information about the status of the rails ahead.

Such was the state of things on the cold night of January 15, 1909, as two trains sped down the tracks beside the Colorado River near Dotsero, about fifteen miles east of Glenwood Springs. The westbound Denver & Rio Grande No. 5 was a passenger train with engineer Gustaf "Gus" Olson at the helm. Olson was an experienced engineer with a clean safety record. His conductor was Albert McCurdy. In addition to an engine and tender, the No. 5 included a baggage car, smoking car, dining car, chair car, tourist sleeping car, and a full complement of Pullman sleepers.

Olson and McCurdy had been notified that a two-engine freight train would be leaving Glenwood Springs at about the same time their No. 5 was heading west into the canyon. Gus Olson was instructed to pull the passenger train into a siding at Dotsero and wait until 9:55 P.M., to allow the freight train to pass by.

In an odd twist of fate, Olson's brother, Sig Olson, was running the freight train. It had indeed left Glenwood Springs on time and was speeding east through Glenwood Canyon.

As No. 5, the passenger train, approached Dotsero, Gus Olson checked his watch. He later said that he misread the time by ten minutes. He thought he had time to make it to another siding about five miles west of Dotsero. Conductor McCurdy, who was in the caboose, noticed that the train didn't slow at Dotsero as directed. He immediately signaled engineer Olson to stop the train. Seconds later, McCurdy saw the headlights of the oncoming freight train.

The collision occurred at a curve near the entrance to Glenwood Canyon between Dotsero and Spruce Creek. Seconds before impact, the engineers and some trainmen jumped from their trains. A fireman on the freight train crew, John Anderson, reported later, "I was turning with my shovel toward the tender when the glare of a headlight shone in my eyes. There was but one thing to do and that was to leap. There was too much excitement to remember where I landed. My first thought, as in the case of the engineers, was to assist the injured passengers."

The impact was terrific, smashing the engines of both trains, compacting them together into a mass of iron and steel. Pieces of debris were scattered over a huge area. Steam hissed from the engines, and at least two fires broke out. On train No. 5, the smoking car partially derailed, but miraculously none of the sleeper cars left the track. One car telescoped into the chair car and smashed it into small pieces. Most of the deaths and injuries occurred there, as passengers in it were crushed by debris or thrown from the train.

The force of the collision crushed the two locomotives into one another. PHOTOGRAPH COURTESY OF THE EAGLE COUNTY HISTORICAL SOCIETY.

Despite pitch-black darkness and freezing temperatures, uninjured passengers in the rear cars acted quickly. Some used shovels to throw snow on the engines to put out fires. Others, guided only by two train lanterns, went to the aid of passengers crying out in the dark. Twenty-one people were killed and forty more injured, some very seriously. (Seven of the injured passengers died within a week.)

One passenger, Blanche McKibbon of Memphis, Nebraska, was riding in the observation car on train No. 5. The collision threw her to the floor, but she was unhurt. After a night of turmoil, she wrote a letter to her sister, creating for posterity a firsthand account of the wreck. In her letter, McKibbon noted that the newspaper reports "really are not very accurate," and went on in remarkable detail. "I ran along the track," she wrote, "and met a man all blackened and bleeding about the face carrying a suitcase. When we met, he put out his hand and said, 'My God girl, you cannot go up there, it's too awful.' I could hear the groaning and screaming and shouting and blows of axes." McKibbon and other passengers cleared broken dishes from the dining car, which was otherwise in good shape, and brought in mattresses and linens from the Pullman cars. Then "the terrible work began." She explained, "There was a young doctor who was a wonder—my, how he worked and how levelheaded he was. He cared for so many so quickly. Fortunately, he had morphine and [a] hypodermic needle and soon had many quiet so we could at least hear." Another doctor (a woman) arrived to help, and then the young man went to work on the injured in the wreckage itself. Soon, he sent word back to the dining car that he wanted "that little dark haired nurse" (meaning McKibbon). Here her description grew more graphic.

We reached the baggage car and before I went in, several men tried to stop me and asked if I could stand it, so I was prepared and was glad to be so useful. . . . [I]n every corner were groaning, writhing, bleeding figures. My feet stuck to the floor in blood and the first thing I heard was, "Oh sister, can't you help me?" It was one of the firemen; the doctor beckoned and the next few hours are beyond description. I saw three die—two men and a little boy. One woman's face was crushed to a pulp and one leg broken and one badly sprained and internal injuries. She died later.

Rescuers removed bodies from the wreckage and laid them side by side along the tracks. They tended to the injured as best they could through the night. Early the next morning, a relief train arrived from Glenwood Springs with doctors and nurses on board. They relieved the exhausted caretakers, and most of the dead and injured were loaded onto the relief train and taken to Glenwood Springs. The dead, many still unidentified, were sent to the morgue, and the injured were taken to the county hospital and sanitarium. When those beds were full, victims were taken to hotels.

Among those hospitalized was passenger train engineer Gus Olson. He had serious internal injuries, and doctors worried he wouldn't survive. His brother Sig, who had jumped from the freight engine, was bruised and battered but on the mend.

There were not enough surgeons in Glenwood Springs to deal with the huge influx of the injured, but as news of the disaster spread, doctors from surrounding communities came to Glenwood Springs to assist.

The wreck etched tales of tragedy across many lives. In one case, an entire family was killed except for a three-month-old baby who was injured. A local family adopted the baby. In another case, Mr. and Mrs. Kettle of Ashton, Nebraska, were killed, but two of their children, aged two and four, survived. Three other members of the Kettle family also perished.

A number of children were killed or orphaned that night. One young boy's story at least had a "silver lining." The Eagle County coroner, Dr. Joseph Gilpin, arrived at the wreck site the following morning. He attended to the injured, including a boy who was bleeding from a nasty head wound. Dr. Gilpin had a kindly demeanor and a long white beard, earning him the nickname of "Doctor Santa" among the local children. The boy confided in him, saying that he could not find his mother. Sadly, the doctor learned that she was dead and her body had already been taken to a morgue in Glenwood Springs. The boy then explained that his mother had sewed all their money into the hem of her dress for safekeeping. With the boy patched up, Dr. Gilpin accompanied him into town and to the morgue. All of the torn and bloodstained clothing had been thrown into a heap, but the boy identified his mother's dress. The money was recovered just before the victims' clothing was to be burned.

In all, twenty-one people died in the wreck, another five succumbed to their injuries in the week that followed, and thirty more suffered significant injuries. Of the dead, many were from Colorado and Nebraska, but some were from as far away as Pennsylvania and Washington, D.C.

As coroner, Dr. Gilpin impaneled a jury mostly from the nearby town of Gypsum to investigate the scene of the accident. On January 23, more than 100 people jammed into the coroner's inquest, held in Red Cliff, the county seat at the time. Dr. Gilpin and District Attorney Hogan examined witnesses, and another attorney, Charles Darrow of Glenwood Springs, represented the railroad company. Reporters arrived from the *Denver Post*, *Leadville Herald Democrat*, and *Grand Junction Sentinel*.

The first person to testify was Hugh Wilson, an assistant division superintendent for the Denver & Rio Grande, who explained the order that had been given to the two trains. The nature of the order was corroborated by a train dispatcher: passenger train No. 5 was to wait at the Dotsero siding until 9:55 P.M. to allow the freight train to safely pass. Such orders are sent in duplicate. The conductor was expected to read the order and give the duplicate to the engineer. The order was then passed down and read by the fireman, brakeman, and flagman.

The No. 5 conductor, McCurdy, testified that he had read the order, and, when the train did not stop at Dotsero, he pulled the bell cord to alert the engineer, Gus Olson, to stop. McCurdy said that Olson applied air brakes, reducing the speed of the train to twenty-five miles per hour before the collision. He added that the emergency brakes were not applied. The brakeman corroborated McCurdy's account.

The jury deliberated only fifty-one minutes before finding engineer Gus Olson guilty of the deaths of twenty-one people by "disobeying orders through negligence or some unknown cause." The district attorney, however, declined to prosecute due to a lack of conclusive evidence, saying a trial would be a waste of taxpayer money.

In the aftermath of the tragedy, conductor McCurdy quit the railroad, and engineer Gus Olson moved to Los Angeles to recover from his injuries and escape publicity. Newspapers demanded increased safety measures from the railroad.

The 1909 train disaster at Dotsero and several other accidents on Colorado rails the same year—causing a total of 113 fatalities and 116 injuries—led the Colorado Railroad Commission to examine railway safety laws. In its annual report of December 31, 1909, the commission wrote that such a great loss of life in a single year was "painful and alarming." It further strongly recommended implementing a system of block signals throughout the state rail network. That solution was eventually mandated by law, and within a decade, railroad timetables abided by standardized time zones, greatly improving rail safety some sixty years after the start of rail travel in Colorado.

SOURCES

Train Wreck at Eden, 1904

"Eden, CO Train Disaster, Aug 1904." GenDisasters.com.

Helmers, Dow. *Tragedy At Eden*. Swallow Press, 1971.

"The Last Watchman, The Lost Story of Colorado's Worst Train Wreck." *Pueblo Pulp*, April 24, 2018.

"Over One Hundred Lives Lost in Train Wreck Near Pueblo." *Alamosa Journal*, August 12, 1904.

Taylor, Jack. "Colorado History: The Eden Train Wreck." KEKB 99.9 Grand Junction, October 16, 2018.

"Worst Train Wreck in the History of the D. & R. G." *Telluride Journal*, August 8, 1904.

Dotsero Train Collision, 1909

"21 Meet Death in Train Wreck on D. & R. G. RR." *Los Angeles Herald*, January 17, 1909.

"Awful Wreck on D. & R. G. Railroad." *Dolores Star*, January 22, 1909.

"Description of a Scene by a Nebraska Traveler." *Nebraska State Journal*, January 28, 1909.

Fillmore, J. D. "Coroner's Jury Render Verdict at Inquest on Deaths of Dotsero Victims." *Eagle County Blade*, January 28, 1909.

Heicher, Kathy. *Eagle County Characters: Historic Tales of a Mountain Valley*. The History Press, 2013.

Heicher, Kathy. "Mountains, Men, & Memories: Death and Destruction in Dotsero." *Vail Daily*, January 17, 2018.

"Twenty-one Dead, Forty Hurt in Colorado Wreck." *The New York Times*, January 17, 1909.

"Twenty-one Killed in Wreck on the Rio Grande." *Nebraska State Journal*, January 17, 1909.

Varney, Philip. *Ghost Towns of Colorado*. Voyageur Press, 1999.

CHAPTER 4

COAL, OIL, AND GAS EXPLOSIONS

COLORADO IS RICH IN FOSSIL FUELS, SO THE ATTENDANT INDUSTRIES are highly visible in the Centennial State. They procure the raw materials that drive much of modern society and also provide jobs for many Coloradoans. But extraction and processing can be a risky business, and when things go wrong, the outcomes are sometimes dramatic and often deadly.

HASTINGS MINE EXPLOSION, 1916

In the late 1800s and early 1900s, coal was one of Colorado's most important natural resources. It fueled railroad locomotives and ore-smelting furnaces and heated homes and businesses. The huge steelwork foundries in Pueblo ran on Colorado coal. By 1917, at least 238 coal mines were operating in Colorado, including several in the 1,100-square-mile Trinidad coalfield, which is part of the larger Raton Mesa coal region of southern Colorado and northern New Mexico. The coal beds throughout this region are rich in methane, which is released during the mining process. When methane and other flammable gases build up in a mine, the risk of fire and explosion becomes acute.

Because coal was a major fuel for trains (as well as other things), coal mining and railroads often existed in tandem; many coal towns were also railroad towns and vice versa. Such was the case for Trinidad and its satellite communities, including Ludlow, thirteen miles north, and Hastings, on a spur line two miles west of Ludlow. The Hastings Mine was operated by the Victor-American Fuel Company, the oldest coal company in Colorado. It was owned by John Cleveland Osgood, who was vehemently opposed to labor unions and thought that company owners knew best how to take care of employees.

The Hastings site consisted of the mine itself, 100 ovens for converting coal into coke, and a camp or town housing more than 1,000 people. By 1910, Hastings boasted a school, church, store, meat market, and saloon. The mine featured two main shafts, A and B, following coal seams at a 5 percent downward slope directly into the mountainside for about three-quarters of a mile. About halfway along their length, the shafts were connected by a cross tunnel. The main workings of the B seam were about 8,000 feet below the mountaintop. In the main shafts, an electric mining machine cut the coal. To prevent dangerous gas buildup, the whole network was ventilated by an eight-foot-diameter Sirocco fan capable of moving more than 90,000 cubic feet of air per minute.

The Hastings Mine (and Charles Niccoli Saloon), seen here in 1914, were beehives of activity during coal's heydays. PHOTOGRAPH BY LOUIS CHARLES MCCLURE, COURTESY OF THE DENVER PUBLIC LIBRARY, SPECIAL COLLECTIONS, MCC 4296.

Most miners were paid not by the hour but based on how much coal they produced. At the Hastings Mine in 1917, the rate was $0.58 per ton, or about $3.25 for an average day's work.

The work was dangerous, and Hastings had already tasted tragedy. During a shift in June 1912, a night watchman saw smoke billowing out of the entrance to the mine. He alerted rescuers, who were able to save one badly injured miner. Twelve others suffocated to death. Investigators blamed improperly placed charges or the wrong kind or quantity of explosives. This could create what was called a "windy shot," which expends its force on the mine air, igniting coal dust or gas and causing a larger explosion.

Working conditions at the Hastings Mine improved somewhat over the next few years. Then, at the end of March 1916, despite Osgood's anti-union stance, the Victor-American Fuel Company signed a three-year operating agreement with the United Mine Workers of America. The future looked bright.

Snow was falling at six thirty on the morning of Friday, April 27, 1917, when the fire boss entered the mine to ensure that it was clear of methane gas and other hazards. After he gave the all clear, 122 miners and company men (track layers, timber framers, fire bosses, etc.) went to work. It began as a typical day, the miners loading coal into wooden cars that were pulled upslope with a single cable to the surface. One man, Frank Millatto, rode with the cars of coal. He had just completed a second trip to the surface and was returning into the mine when he heard a signal to stop the cars. Looking ahead, he could see smoke. Realizing that a fire had ignited in the mine, he got out of the coal car to sound an alarm. Just then an explosion ripped through the mine deep underground. Millatto was the only person working that shift who survived.

Hearing the alarm, the mine superintendent and a rescue crew of five men headed into the mine, but they quickly retreated in the face of fierce heat and dense smoke. Almost immediately, another rescue crew tried to enter the mine but was also forced back. It appeared that, after the explosion, a sheet of flame swept through the mine, killing most of the men instantly. Those not killed by the fire died beneath falling timbers and rock or suffocated.

From the very beginning, the mine superintendent, D. J. Griffith, said it would be a miracle if rescue teams found anyone alive. Information regarding the explosion and rescue efforts could be conveyed only over the one telephone line connecting the mine with the town of Trinidad, so little news was readily available. The first rescuers on the scene were unable to reach the spot where most of the miners had been working because, in addition to the heat and fire, the explosion had blown out the walls and ceiling of the main slope, blocking their way and leaving wreckage everywhere. Lumber and canvas needed to repair sections so that rescuers could safely enter had to be carried on men's backs for three-quarters of a mile.

As word of the disaster spread, relatives of the men in the mine began to congregate at the mine site. Wives, sons, and daughters gathered, many speaking and praying in their native languages. Some of these family members went home again to get out of the freezing cold caused by a winter storm. National Guardsmen were stationed at the mine entrance.

Throughout the first day and on following days, men from the nearby Delagua and Berwind Mines came to offer help. The *Rocky Mountain News* reported that almost every mine in Las Animas and Huerfano Counties was represented in the rescue efforts, and miners came from Dawson, New Mexico, where only four years earlier 263 men had died in the Stag Canyon Mine explosion. It soon became apparent, however, that there was no hope of rescue—and the effort of recovering bodies proved painfully slow.

It was Monday morning, April 30, before a Colorado Bureau of Mines rescue crew arrived from Golden. The four-man crew included a mining engineer and three trained rescue miners with special equipment. So-called "helmet crews," named for their oxygen masks, which resembled deep-sea diving helmets, worked about 400 feet ahead of the rescue crew, clearing the way for them. The men had to remove rockfall and repair broken timbers to restore ventilation within the mine. When they finally did reach the main group of victims, rescuers reported finding some bodies in a kneeling position with coats pulled over their heads, as if they were guarding themselves from the deadly fumes. Some victims were burned so badly that they were identifiable only by the numbered, brass identification tags, called checks, carried by each miner. The checks corresponded to a matching check and each miner's name left at the surface on a large board. Some miners carried their checks in their pockets, but others put them in their lunch boxes or jackets, which they sometimes removed while working. Some Hastings victims could not be identified because their checks weren't on their bodies.

On May 6, a rescuer named Walter Kerr collapsed and died while carrying a body. An autopsy revealed that Kerr, who was twenty-seven and a member of the Berwind CF&I Mine helmet crew, had a "defective" heart. The strain of heavy work while wearing a breathing apparatus was too much for him. By May 10, crews had recovered 101 bodies. Four months later, another 16 bodies had been recovered and identified. Four of the miners who were on shift April 27 were never recovered. Most of the victims were buried in either the Catholic or Masonic cemeteries in Trinidad, where sometimes five or more funerals were held in a single day. The Greek victims were buried about four miles from Hastings in the Knights of Pythias Cemetery.

A coroner's inquest determined that the mine inspector and instructor of safety, David Reese, caused the explosion when he struck a match to relight his Wolf safety lamp, which was used to test for the presence of gas in the mine. Presumably, as an inspector Reese had a key to open the locked lamp so he could relight it, but that could be done safely only at the surface outside the mine. But miners sometimes picked the lamp lock and risked relighting the flame underground rather than lose digging time (and therefore pay) while walking to the surface. As an inspector, Reese had been schooled against precisely such a risk.

Reese's body was found on May 10 at the main south entry. Although a spent match was not found, there were twenty-two matches in Reese's pocket. State law prohibited matches in mines where safety lamps were used. Miners entering the mines were often searched for matches, but a mine inspector himself would not have been searched.

When a juror at the inquest asked Victor-American Mine superintendent Griffith how this could have happened, Griffith said, "This is something that I can't make out. What made him to do such a thing? Of course we thought the lamp was absolutely safe in his hands. He was a good, careful man, and absolutely practical." Griffith was not the only one surprised by this finding. Reese was well known and respected throughout the mining community; such a lapse in his diligence was hard to imagine. In September 1919, the Colorado state mining inspector issued an order prohibiting the use of key-locking safety lamps in coal mines.

The state used its new workmen's compensation law for the first time to pay the dependents of victims of the disaster. Relatives of the victims received a total of $147,650. Under the law, only dependents were entitled to receive insurance money, and the most a single family could collect was $2,500. The families of forty-one victims who were U.S. citizens each received $2,500, but the families of fifty-four victims who weren't citizens received only $800 each. Twenty-six of the victims had no dependents, so only burial expenses of $75 each were paid. In all, 144 children lost their fathers on that single day.

The workers in the Hastings Mine were mostly foreign-born. Among the 121 killed in the explosion were men from Greece, Australia, Italy, Mexico, Poland, Wales, Spain, and Serbia. Another 27 were American. Two of the victims were only sixteen years old; the oldest was fifty-eight.

The explosion marked the end of an era for the Hastings Mine. Within seven months of the explosion, the town's population decreased drastically. In 1917, the Hastings Mine produced 74,221 tons of coal, but output fell to 7,049 tons by 1923. Eventually, the mine was abandoned and the portal was sealed with cement. By 1929, the population of Hastings had dropped to 300 people. A final cleanup was not done until 1952. Today, a small memorial marks the site on County Road 44, just a short distance west of the Ludlow Monument.

The April 27, 1917, Hastings Mine explosion remains the deadliest mining disaster in Colorado history.

CONOCO OIL REFINERY BLAST, 1978

Colorado is rich in mineral, oil, and gas deposits, so the extraction industry has a presence, more tangible in some places than others. Still, when most people think of oil refineries and gas wells they probably don't envision them in close proximity to metro areas and residential neighborhoods.

That puzzling pairing, however, makes the following two disasters in this chapter all the more terrifying.

Originally built in 1940, the Continental Oil Company (Conoco) refinery in Commerce City manufactured gasoline, butane, and propane. By 1978, the plant supplied about 15 percent of the Denver area's petroleum products. The sprawling plant included refinery facilities and a number of large storage tanks with a total capacity of 1.5 million barrels—all of which sat just ten minutes northeast of downtown Denver.

On October 3, 1978, a small night crew had almost finished its shift, and the eastern sky was brightening just before dawn. Suddenly, at 6:33 A.M., a huge explosion rocked the plant, shooting an orange fireball 500 feet into the air. This was followed by flames and billowing smoke. The explosion registered 3.5 on the Richter scale at the Regis College observatory in Denver and magnitude 1.5 at the U.S. Geological Survey offices in Golden. It was heard throughout the entire Denver metropolitan area and shook houses miles away.

Local fire departments arrived before the 6:56 A.M. sunrise and had the blaze contained by 11 A.M., though flames continued to burn through the afternoon. The plant personnel manager, Gary Thomas, was on-site when the explosion hit. "I started running," Thomas said. "There was one massive explosion." He later identified the three people who died: Steve French, David Hobbs, and Ron DeHerrera. Another eleven were injured and rushed to local hospitals in serious or critical condition. Because the blast occurred so early in the day, only this handful of the plant's 160 employees were working at the time. If the blast had occurred during the day shift, the number of fatalities and injuries would have been much higher. Several smaller explosions occurred while firefighters fought the blaze, and one fireman was injured. Firefighters were able to keep the flames away from nearby petroleum storage tanks, the closest of which was only 200 feet from the blaze.

A $2.5 million gasoline-production unit, which had been completed only two weeks earlier, was at the center of the explosion. Investigators with the U.S. Occupational Safety and Health Administration suspected that fumes or vapor leaking from the new gasoline unit had ignited, and they noted that the plant was not equipped with a vapor-detection system. The destruction from the explosion prevented investigators from pinpointing the exact ignition source.

The plant manager, Robert Alexander, said the initial explosion was touched off by leaking, flammable fumes. He said that at least nine employees were in the immediate blast zone, and before the blast they had reported fumes and called in a company fire engine as a precaution.

After the explosion, a man claiming to be a Conoco employee called the Adams County sheriff's department and said he had planted a bomb near a storage tank at the oil refinery. But searchers found no sign of one.

Firefighters spray water on the smoldering wreckage of the Conoco refinery in Commerce City. PHOTOGRAPH COURTESY OF THE DENVER PUBLIC LIBRARY, SPECIAL COLLECTIONS, WH2129.

The powerful blast blew windows and doors—and even steel siding—off buildings. PHOTOGRAPH COURTESY OF THE DENVER PUBLIC LIBRARY, SPECIAL COLLECTIONS, WH2129.

Reporters who viewed the site said it looked like a war zone, with smoke, fire, twisted pieces of steel, and buildings with doors and sides blown off. In the neighborhoods surrounding the refinery, more than forty businesses and homes reported structural damage, and windows were broken at many more. Alexander, the plant manager, said that the refinery was "twenty-five percent destroyed," with damages estimated at $5 million.

Conoco soon announced plans to rebuild the refinery, at a cost of $22.5 million. The plant reopened on Memorial Day weekend in 1979 and was fully reconstructed by the end of 1980. By that time, it was back to its former capacity of 32,000 barrels of crude oil a day. A Canadian company later bought Conoco and all of its facilities, including this refinery. It continues to operate in Commerce City as the Suncor Refinery and processes 98,000 barrels of oil a day.

FIRESTONE HOME EXPLOSION, 2017

The community of Firestone, Colorado, nestles on the rolling prairie in southern Weld County, about eight miles due east of Longmont. Here, Mark and Erin Martinez had a home at 6312 Twilight Avenue in the Oak Meadows subdivision and enjoyed a happy life with their two children, Nathan and Jaelynn, and two dogs, Carmella and Little Guy. Mark was a licensed plumber and a supervisor with the local public works department. Erin taught science at Mountain Range High School in nearby Westminster.

On the afternoon of April 17, 2017, Mark and his brother-in-law Joey Irwin were installing a new hot-water heater in the basement of the Martinez's home. Joey was Erin's brother; he and Mark had graduated from Frederick High School together in 1992 and had remained close friends. Joey mentored Mark on hunting trips, and the two enjoyed fishing together. Joey was also a master plumber. Neither of the two men had any reason to suspect the hidden danger that was lurking in the basement with them that day.

At 4:45 P.M., a tremendous explosion ripped through the Martinez home, instantly killing Mark and Joey. The east side of the house crumbled, and the entire two-story home tilted sharply to that side. Erin was trapped on the main floor under the collapsed roof. A construction crew working at a nearby apartment complex rushed to the burning home and used a forklift to hoist the debris. A neighbor, Ben Chapman, also ran to help. "She was in there kind of deeper than the forklift could reach," Chapman said. "So we were all in there just kind of pulling boards and drywall chunks, and just trying to free her manually." Erin's son, Nathan, was upstairs when the blast hit, and he escaped by jumping from a window. Jaelynn wasn't at home at the time.

The Martinez home was quickly engulfed in flames after the blast. PHOTOGRAPH BY DENNIS HERRERA.

After the explosion and blaze, little remained of the Martinez home. PHOTOGRAPH BY DENNIS HERRERA.

Erin was airlifted to a hospital in critical condition. Firefighters battled the flames, but the blaze completely consumed the home. The day after the explosion, a search crew pulled the bodies of Mark and Joey from the charred rubble. The couple's dogs also died in the blast.

In the days that followed, investigators combed through the demolished house and soon discovered the cause of the explosion and fire. As Ted Poszywak, chief of the Frederick-Firestone Fire Protection District, said, "It was an unusual and tragic set of circumstances." The homes in Oak Meadows had been built on top of an old oil and gas field owned and operated by Texas-based Anadarko Petroleum Corporation. Regulations stipulated that homes had to be set back at least 150 feet from any gas wells, and investigators discovered that one natural gas well, which had been drilled in 1993, was 178 feet from the Martinez's home. State records revealed that the well had been shut down in 2016 and then reopened in January 2017. But investigators soon discovered an abandoned one-inch pipe—a "flowline"—leading from the well. The flowline had been cut, probably when it was inactive, but the broken line was leaking "fugitive gas," which is unrefined and lacks odorants normally added to gas so leaks can be detected.

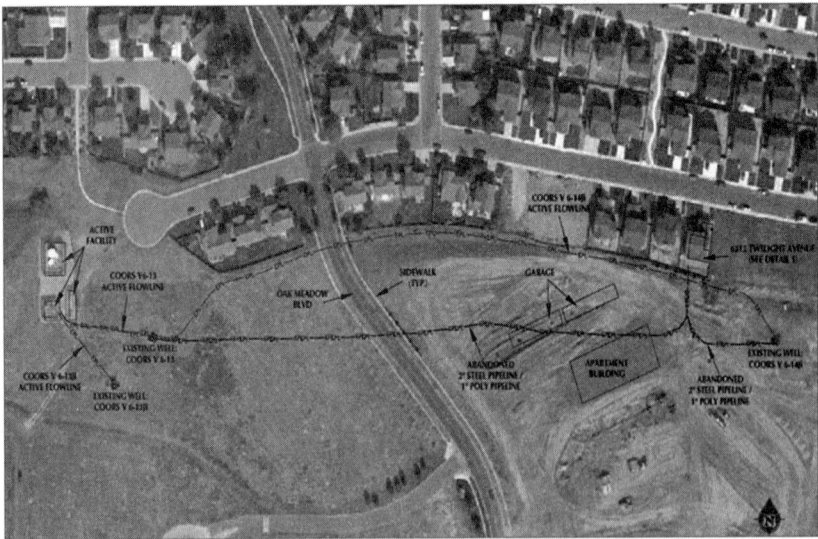

This schematic shows the proximity of gas pipelines to homes in the Firestone neighborhood. The Martinez home is first on the right in the first row next to the graded construction site. PHOTOGRAPH COURTESY OF THE NATIONAL TRANSPORTATION SAFETY BOARD.

Over the span of four months, the gas had permeated the soil six feet from the home's foundation. From there, it entered the Martinez's basement via a French drain and sump pit. Poszywak noted that the flowline had clearly been abandoned, but when it was traced back to the well, its valves were found in the "on" position. Mark Martinez and Joey Irwin had no way of knowing that the basement was full of gas. All that was needed to cause a disaster was an ignition source, perhaps a match or lighter used to fire up a soldering torch to work on the hot-water heater.

On April 27, ten days after the explosion, Anadarko Petroleum Corporation announced that, as a safety precaution, it would close more than 3,000 vertical wells across northeastern Colorado, including the three remaining active wells in Oak Meadows. However, state records showed that Weld County alone had 23,319 active oil and gas wells, about 43 percent of all the wells in Colorado. There was no map showing the locations of all the flowlines tied to those wells. In the years leading up to the Martinez explosion, Weld County had also experienced a housing boom, issuing about 2,500 new home permits a year. This combination of trends was bound to lead to tragedy.

Colorado Governor John Hickenlooper ordered oil and gas operators to inspect and pressure-test flowlines from all working and abandoned natural-gas wells within 1,000 feet of occupied buildings. He said all unused lines had to be marked and capped. Abandoned lines were to be cut below the surface and sealed.

With sudden awareness of the potential for more carnage, people began demanding tighter regulation of Colorado's oil and gas industry. They said that the Colorado Oil and Gas Conservation Commission (COGCC) was too lax in its oversight, and that the risk was clearly more widespread and serious than previously acknowledged. Advocates for improved safety pointed out that the issue would likely grow worse as corrosion and seismic movement continued to damage aging wells and flowlines and as more homes sprouted on the ground above.

U.S. Representative Jared Polis (who became governor of Colorado in January 2019) said, "What occurred in Firestone, while devastating, was predictable because Colorado sadly does not have adequate protections against dangerous oil and gas developments in our neighborhoods. The days when oil and gas profits are valued more than Coloradoans' safety, property, and quality of life need to end."

Within weeks of the blast, Twilight Avenue residents Jeffrey and Karla Baum filed a lawsuit against Anadarko, the subdivision developer, and the homebuilder, alleging negligence for allowing the broken flowline to leak gas into the neighborhood. That suit was dismissed in October 2017, and the Baums' attorneys appealed, adding a group of Oak Meadows homeowners to the list of plaintiffs and dropping the developer and homebuilder as defendants. A group of Anadarko shareholders also sued the company, claiming stock losses tied to Anadarko's "lip service" to safety and the subsequent home explosion. These lawsuits have not yet been resolved.

On May 16, 2017, Firestone residents gathered to honor Mark Martinez and recognize him for his dedication to the community in his role with public works and as a volunteer softball coach. His daughter, other relatives, and friends attended, but his wife, Erin, was still hospitalized in serious condition. Meanwhile, Anadarko offered methane-detecting equipment to residents of the neighborhood.

In 2018, Erin Martinez reached an undisclosed settlement with Anadarko. Her children wanted to stay close to their friends in Firestone, so Erin searched for a home far from any oil or gas wells and lines. "Months later, I saw crews from the oil and gas industry digging and searching for an abandoned well behind my house," she recounted. "They kept getting closer and closer to my property line. They finally located the well in my neighbor's backyard along the fence line that we share. As a result . . . we are in the process of moving again. And I am trying to get my son to trust that this time, it will be okay."

In August 2019, Anadarko was acquired by Occidental Petroleum, with $10 billion in financial backing from businessman Warren Buffett.

The National Transportation Safety Board (NTSB) finally published its report on the Firestone gas explosion on October 29, 2019. It determined that the probable cause was a natural-gas leak through a flowline that had been severed during the construction of the home in 2015. The report also blamed the government of Firestone for allowing development on former oil and gas fields without full knowledge of underground flowline locations. The report stated, "None of the three lines found at the residence were properly abandoned in accordance with . . . requirements."

COGCC regulators had waited for the NTSB report before taking punitive action against the oil company. In March 2020, the COGCC announced that it would seek an enforcement penalty of $18.25 million, the largest by tenfold of any ever sought by the commission. COGCC's director, Jeff Robbins, said that "the aggravating factor of death," which had never before been applied, boosted the fine amount.

Occidental Petroleum announced that it would not contest the penalty and noted that part of it would be used "to fund projects designed to strengthen safety and best practices for the industry and for all Coloradoans living near oil and gas operations."

In response, Erin Martinez said, "No amount of penalty or fine is ever going to take away our immense pain and suffering nor bring Mark and Joey back. We have to wake up every morning and go to bed every night living with this horrific nightmare. Our lives are forever changed. It is hard to comprehend that the only recourse is a penalty or fine; how do you put a price on human life? However, legally that is all that can be done." Erin said that the passage of time has only worsened the pain of losing her husband and brother as a result of Anadarko's "extreme negligence."

But Erin channeled that pain into at least one positive outcome; she spearheaded an effort to turn the vacant lot at 6312 Twilight Avenue into a park honoring the two men. Two Hunters Park was dedicated on November 6, 2020. It features sculpted metal pheasants and fish in memory of Mark and Joey's passion for hunting and fishing. A central oak tree shades concrete etched with images of camping, fishing, and chess, as well as Nathan and Jaelynn's handprints. Erin said she hopes the park "can represent what our home represented: a loving place where everyone was welcome, lots of laughter and lots of smiles. I want that to be invoked again, because that's what we shared with Mark and the kids there."

SOURCES

Hastings Mine Explosion, 1917

"1917 Hastings Mine Disaster, Hastings Colorado." By user JerryMiner, Mine Forum, last modified February 4, 2015.

Hedlund, Mark. "Hastings, Colorado." *Encyclopedia of Forlorn Places*, August 19, 2019.

"Hundred and twenty men perish in mine explosion." *Ogden Examiner*, April 28, 1917.

Montgomery, Mellanee. 1917 Hastings Mine Disaster blog, 2018.

Paul, Jesse. "A 1917 coal mine explosion in southern Colorado killed 121. But it's just a faint memory in the state's history." *Denver Post*, April 27, 2017.

"Thirteen men killed in mine explosion today." Fort Collins *Weekly Courier*, June 21, 1912.

Conoco Oil Refinery Blast, 1978

Associated Press. "Explosion kills four, injures 11." *Daily Kent Stater*, October 4, 1978.

"Commerce City—1978." *Denver Fire Journal & Western Fire History*, January 31, 2018.

Rogers, James. "Continental Oil Refinery Explosion and Fire." Events, Research News. Denver Public Library, October 4, 2018.

Firestone Home Explosion, 2017

Aguilar, John. "Federal report on fatal Firestone explosion blames gas leak, government approval to build homes without pipeline maps." *Denver Post*, October 29, 2019.

Aguilar, John. "$18 million fine proposed in fatal Firestone home explosion." *Denver Post*, March 12, 2020.

Boyce, Dan. "Fatal home explosion in Firestone reignites setback debate." *Greeley Tribune*, May 7, 2017, updated May 13, 2020.

"Deadly Firestone home explosion caused by gas from cut, abandoned line to well." Fox 31 Denver, May 2, 2017.

Hammon, Kelsey. "Site of Firestone house explosion transformed into commemorative park for victims." *Greeley Tribune*, November 23, 2020.

Hickey, Chuck. "Coroner identifies men killed in Firestone house explosion, fire." Fox 31 Denver, April 20, 2017.

Hood, Grace. "2 Years After A House Exploded Near A Firestone Oil and Gas Well, the Federal Report is Finally Here." Colorado Public Radio, October 29, 2019.

"'I Remember Being Blown into the Air': Erin Martinez Describes Firestone Home Explosion, Calls for Oil & Gas Changes." CBS 4 Denver, February 28, 2019.

Ingold, John. "Anadarko faces investor lawsuit over Firestone house explosion." *Denver Post*, May 26, 2017.

Kelly, David. "Deadly house explosion in Colorado traced to uncapped pipe from gas well." *Los Angeles Times*, May 2, 2017.

"Pipeline Accident Brief: Natural Gas Explosion at Family Residence, Firestone, Colorado, April 17, 2017." National Transportation Safety Board, NTSB/PAB-19/02.

"Timeline of Fatal Gas Explosion at House In Firestone." CBS 4 Denver, June 4, 2017.

CHAPTER 5

HAILSTORMS

HAIL IS AN AWFUL FACT OF LIFE EACH YEAR FOR FARMERS ON THE plains from Alberta, Canada, to eastern New Mexico. Even if their crops have survived drought, winds, insects, and winter cold, farmers may yet lose their harvest to hail. Each year, hailstorms cause millions of dollars in agricultural losses. No other part of the country gets more frequent or severe hailstorms, and Colorado is right in the middle of it. And of course the losses are not restricted to crops. Hailstorms severely disrupt transportation and daily life. Large hail can damage cars, homes, businesses, and structures of all kinds. In some cases, hail has killed livestock and people.

Meteorologist Kari Bowen with the National Weather Service in Boulder, Colorado, says that the ingredients for a hailstorm include instability, a high dew point, a strong updraft, and a trigger. The dew point is the temperature at which water vapor condenses into droplets. A higher (that is, warmer) dew point means that humidity is high—the air holds a lot of water. An updraft occurs when air masses of different temperatures mix, creating upward energy. When Colorado's unique geography and weather conditions are just right, they can generate spectacular hailstorms. Some of these are major disasters.

Hailstones form when strong updrafts inside thunderclouds carry water droplets up into colder air, where the droplets freeze. The frozen pellets start to fall, only to be carried up again. Each time the pellets cycle from lower, wet, warmer air back up to colder air, a layer of ice is added. When pellets reach 0.2 inch in diameter, they're classified as hailstones. Gravity pulls them downward, but if updrafts in the thunderstorm keep tumbling the hailstones upward, they can grow as big as golf balls, baseballs, or larger. When the hailstones get large and heavy enough that the storm's updrafts can't support them, they fall to the ground. Larger hailstones tend to fall at a higher speed, with three-inch stones reaching 110 miles per hour. Many hailstorms last for only a few minutes, but some continue for twenty minutes or longer.

The 625-square-mile region where the borders of Colorado, Wyoming, and Nebraska intersect is known as Hail Alley. Each year, an average of nine to eleven hailstorms strike there, more than anywhere else in North America. Fort Collins is right in the middle of

Some large hailstones are solid ice. Others, like the one shown here, are aggregates of smaller hailstones that clump together. PHOTOGRAPH COURTESY OF THE NATIONAL OCEANIC AND ATMOSPHERIC ADMINISTRATION, NATIONAL SEVERE STORMS LABORATORY.

Hail Alley, and metro Denver, just to the south, is also often hit with severe thunderstorms and hail. Nationwide, from 2000 to 2019, insured losses due to hail averaged $8 billion to $14 billion a year. From 2017 through 2019, Colorado ranked second only to Texas for hail loss insurance claims.

These devastating storms can occur any time in spring or summer, but the last week in July and first week of August seem especially prone to severe storms. Some climatologists refer to this timeframe as the "magic window."

The window was wide open on Monday, July 30, 1979. That afternoon, a twenty-minute hailstorm hit Fort Collins, and parts of town saw hailstones the size of grapefruit. Some hailstones crashed right through roofs and into living rooms. One Colorado State University researcher estimated that some of the larger hailstones were traveling at more than 100 miles per hour.

The hail smashed through windows, dented vehicles, and cut through carports. Greenhouses were left in bits and pieces. Hardest hit was the Shields neighborhood southwest of downtown. Huge hailstones damaged 2,000 homes and 2,500 cars, and at least twenty-five people were injured. Several people suffered head injuries, and others had cuts and bruises on their hands and arms, which they had raised to protect their heads and faces. More than twenty people sought treatment at what was then Poudre Valley Memorial Hospital.

One eighty-four-year-old woman was hit by a large hailstone that split open her arm and broke the bone. Most critically injured was Joleen Kappelman. The three-month-old girl was struck in the head by a hailstone while in the arms of her mother, who was hurrying from their car to seek shelter in a McDonald's restaurant. The little one was taken to a hospital, but she did not awaken after surgery. In spite of being placed on life support, the baby girl died of her injuries on August 7.

On July 5, 2019, another severe hailstorm hit Fort Collins. This storm was traveling east at about twenty-two miles per hour, and it produced hail for about four hours. The hailstones averaged 1.6 inches in diameter, but stones up to 2.5 inches were also reported.

The storm broke branches from trees, and leaves and fallen branches littered the sidewalks and streets for days. Residents described broken windows and damaged gutters and siding, ruined gardens, and a huge number of dented cars and broken windshields. A backyard video camera captured pictures of golf-ball-sized hail pounding southeast Fort Collins near Harmony and Timberline. At five o'clock the following morning, thick layers of icy pellets still covered the ground.

Large hail packs a wallop. This storm-chasing vehicle suffered significant damage from hailstones. PHOTOGRAPH COURTESY OF THE NATIONAL OCEANIC AND ATMOSPHERIC ADMINISTRATION, NATIONAL SEVERE STORMS LABORATORY.

Of course, Hail Alley encompasses an area far larger than Fort Collins. A severe thunderstorm with hail hit the metro Denver area on July 11, 1990. The storm developed near Estes Park and traveled southeast, dropping golf-ball-sized hail in a swath five to ten miles wide. The storm moved through the heart of the Denver metro area and then veered toward Colorado Springs. It hit hardest in southwest Boulder, Arvada, Westminster, Wheat Ridge, downtown Denver, Littleton, Lakewood, Castle Rock, and Franktown. Thousands of homes sustained heavy damage to roofs and siding, and tens of thousands of automobiles suffered damage; many were listed as a complete loss. The hail broke traffic signals and streetlights and stripped street signs of their paint. Thousands of trees and shrubs lost their foliage. In many neighborhoods, the hail was so heavy that it clogged drains and flooded streets and basements.

On May 8, 2017, another monstrous hailstorm hit Denver. Most consider it the costliest in Colorado history, with $2.3 billion in damages. This hailstorm hit during the evening rush hour, and hail began piling up like snow on the highway. The official size of the largest hailstone reported to the National Weather Service was 2.75 inches in diameter in Wheat Ridge, though many people reported much larger stones, including several that were photographed on the Metropolitan State College campus.

The Rocky Mountain Insurance Information Association reported that this one storm generated more than 50,000 auto insurance claims and more than 50,000 homeowners insurance claims. Hardest hit areas included Golden, north Lakewood, Wheat Ridge, and northwest Denver. The West Metro Fire Department reported numerous accidents and downed power lines. Small-stream flood advisories were issued for Denver, northwest Adams County, northwest Arapahoe County, and northeast Jefferson County. Flights were delayed at Denver International Airport, and some schools were closed the following day.

The Colorado Mills regional mall was closed due to severe hail damage, including extensive roof damage, broken windows, flooding, and damage to electrical systems.

On September 6, 2019, a severe thunderstorm piled hail on the community of Floyd Hill, causing a mudslide at the top of Clear Creek Canyon.

Windshield damage is one of the more common consequences of getting caught out in a bad hail-storm. PHOTOGRAPH BY SEAN WAUGH, COURTESY OF THE NATIONAL OCEANIC AND ATMOSPHERIC ADMINISTRATION, NATIONAL SEVERE STORMS LABORATORY.

The Colorado State Patrol was forced to close Interstate 70. Two people were rescued from a partly submerged car on Yosemite Street south of Colorado Highway 470. Other vehicles were also stranded in water. The thunderstorm caused problems across the Front Range, including flooding, mudslides, a number of lightning-caused fires, and tornado warnings. Dozens of people at Elitch Gardens Amusement Park were stuck on rides during the hailstorm, and forty-seven were injured by the stones. A tornado touched down at Kipling and 6th Avenue in Lakewood, and a second one struck the Founders Village neighborhood in Castle Rock. Losses totaled more than $6 million.

Hailstorms appear to be getting more destructive. The National Oceanic and Atmospheric Administration reported that, in 2019, hail measuring three inches or more in circumference fell in Colorado, Nebraska, Kansas, and Texas. Severe storms were also reported in South Dakota, Wyoming, and Montana.

Sam Childs, a doctoral student in Colorado State University's atmospheric science department, has predicted more hailstorms with bigger hailstones in Colorado's future. His research shows that reports of hailstones the size of eggs and tennis balls are increasing in number. Childs has noted that small hailstones melt quickly as they fall, but larger hailstones melt less because they fall faster. With a growing percentage of large hailstones, Childs predicts damage will be greater.

Just how big might a hailstone get? Because hailstones usually melt quickly after hitting the ground, it is hard to capture the exact size. The largest officially recorded hailstone in the United States was the size of a small volleyball. It fell to earth near Vivian, South Dakota, on July 23, 2010. The hailstone weighed almost two pounds and left a divot in the ground where it hit. It measured eight inches in diameter, with a circumference of eighteen inches. A rancher picked it up, stored it in a freezer, packed it in dry ice, and shipped it to a lab in Boulder. There, Charles Knight, a hailstone expert, added its dimensions and collection information to a research collection. The giant hailstone was later returned to the rancher.

SOURCES

Doesken, Nolan J. "Hail, Hail, Hail! The Summertime Hazard of Eastern Colorado." *Colorado Climate*, Volume 17, Number 7, April 1994.

Duggan, Kevin. "The 'magic window' of summer weather brought lesser-known 1979 storm." *Coloradoan*, July 27, 2018.

"Fact + Statistics: Hail." Insurance Information Institute, 2021.

Hefty, Jennifer. "Backyard camera video shows hail pelting Southeast Fort Collins on Friday." *Coloradoan*, July 9, 2019.

Nicholson, Kieran. "Hail hits areas north of Denver as stormy weather rolls to the east." *Denver Post*, May 6, 2019.

Reppenhagen, Cory. "Why the Front Range of Colorado is a second 'Hail Alley'." KUSA News 9 Denver, May 8, 2018.

"Supercell Thunderstorms and Hail." Video episode 12 of the *Science of Extreme Weather*. Directed by Eric Snodgrass, distributed by Kanopy, 2006.

Torpey, Jodi. "Colorado's future holds more and bigger hail, CSU weather researcher says." *Denver Post*, June 12, 2019.

CHAPTER 6

LIGHTNING STRIKES

THE UNITED STATES SEES 20 MILLION THUNDERSTORMS EACH YEAR, mostly in spring and summer. Although they vary greatly, a typical thunderstorm is about fifteen miles in diameter and lasts about thirty minutes. When such storms are severe, they may spawn disasters such as floods, mudslides, wildfires, damaging hail, and tornadoes. By definition, thunderstorms generate lightning, which can occur many miles from the storm itself, seemingly out of a clear sky. People may be caught in the open unaware of an approaching storm, or perhaps they're careless of the risk. From 2008 to 2018, Colorado ranked seventh in the nation for lightning-caused fatalities. In a typical year in Colorado, twelve people are injured by lightning and two or three are killed.

Although it ranks high in lightning deaths and injuries, Colorado does not rank high in total number of lightning events. During 2019, Colorado recorded 3.7 million cloud-to-ground lightning strikes and yet ranked only twentieth among all the states. According to *Year of Thunder and Lightning*, an annual report by the Vaisala Group, the top five that year were Texas, Oklahoma, Kansas, Missouri, and Florida. The likely explanation for Colorado's fairly high fatality rate but middling ranking for lightning frequency is twofold: people spend a lot of time outdoors in Colorado, and storms here pop up quickly, especially along the Front Range.

Lightning is a serious hazard for people who work and recreate on Colorado's high mountains, but it strikes more frequently where the mountains meet the plains. No place in Colorado sees more lightning strikes than the Palmer Divide between Denver and Colorado Springs. Researchers Stephen Hodanish of the National Weather Service (NWS) in Pueblo, NWS meteorologist Paul Wolyn, and professor Brandon Vogt of the University of Colorado–Colorado Springs mapped twenty years of lightning strikes. They found that this particular area was more active than most due to three factors: the steep slope of Pikes Peak, which acts as a convector for lightning; the so-called Denver Convergency Velocity Zone, where high-pressure winds from the north meet moist low-pressure fronts off the plains to fuel storms; and the higher elevation of Palmer Divide, which juts out onto the plains. Of course, lightning occurs in other parts of Colorado, too, but not as frequently as in Douglas and El Paso Counties.

Lightning is a beautiful—and dangerous—force of nature. PHOTOGRAPH BY SEAN WAUGH, COURTESY OF VORTEX 2, NATIONAL OCEANIC AND ATMOSPHERIC ADMINISTRATION, NATIONAL SEVERE STORMS LABORATORY.

The three scientists produced a map of cloud-to-ground lightning strikes that occurred from 1996 to 2016. July and August were the most active months, and the most common time of day for strikes was from 3 P.M. to 5 P.M. By far the greatest density of strikes occurred between southeast Denver and Colorado Springs.

The National Weather Service also tracks lightning fatalities in Colorado by county. From 1980 to 2020, lightning killed 100 people in Colorado and injured 487. El Paso and Larimer Counties are neck and neck for lightning casualties, each recording ten deaths. During that same period, El Paso County tallied slightly more injuries, with eighty-four, compared to Larimar County's seventy-six. Other Front Range counties, such as Adams, Arapahoe, Boulder, Denver, Douglas, and Jefferson, also ranked high on the list. Of course, these are among the state's most populated counties, another factor related to high casualty rates; more people mean more chances for someone to be in the wrong place at the wrong time.

The following stories reveal lightning's devastating abruptness and power, and also its seeming capriciousness.

On Tuesday, July 17, 2016, Peter Hawkes, a twenty-three-year-old University of Colorado graduate (originally from New York), and a friend of the same age were golfing in Arvada at the Indian Tree Golf Course. The skies turned dark and a fast-moving thunderstorm hammered the links with rain and lightning. Some golf courses sound a horn to warn golfers of approaching bad weather, but Indian Tree lets golfers decide for themselves when to seek shelter. Witnesses reported four bolts of lightning in the area, one of which struck the course directly.

When the storm struck, Hawkes and his friend took shelter beneath a tree. Lightning hit, and both men fell to the ground. Gene Lucero and his daughter arrived immediately after the strike. The daughter, a lifeguard trained in first aid, began giving Hawkes CPR. A fire truck, police car, and ambulance arrived quickly on the scene. Both of the young golfers were taken to an area hospital. Hawkes was treated in a burn unit for several hours, but he died at 1 A.M. His friend apparently suffered no serious injuries.

Just two days later, on July 19, 2016, lightning caused multiple injuries at the El Paso County Fair in Calhan, thirty-five miles northeast of Colorado Springs. An unidentified woman had just left a building at the north side of the fairgrounds when lightning struck. It hit her and also injured two men near her. Two Air Force Academy firefighters who were volunteering at the medical tent were among the first responders on the scene. They found the woman lying on her back in the dirt. She was bluish-purple and not breathing. They put her on oxygen, and she began breathing on her own. Calhan Fire Department staff arrived and transported the victim via Flight For Life to Swedish Medical Center in Englewood. She suffered third-degree burns, ruptured eardrums, and nerve damage, but doctors expected her to make a full recovery.

People at the fairgrounds reported that, at the time, a storm was visible some distance away, but the sky immediately above them was mostly clear, with only a few clouds. The lightning strike took everyone by surprise.

On Sunday, May 7, 2017, thirty-six-year-old Laura Miller and a fifteen-year-old girl, a family friend, were riding horses on a community bridle trail along Rainbow Creek Road in Sedalia when a storm rolled in around 3:30 P.M. The pair hoped to catch up with Laura's mother, who was riding a few hundred yards ahead, and find shelter. All three were experienced riders, and Laura's mount was an award-winning competitor.

But the storm caught them, and lightning struck a tree about ten feet from the riders. The electricity ran into the ground and then into the animals, killing Miller and her horse instantly. Her mother saw the lightning bolt but not precisely where it hit. A nearby neighbor, Steve Young, recalled hearing three strikes. "The thunder was loud," he said. "You could hear the sizzle." The teenage girl was seriously injured but was conscious and breathing when she was taken to the hospital.

The same storm brought wind with gusts up to sixty-two miles per hour. The wind toppled a tree onto a house in Denver's Park Hill neighborhood and blew down power lines in Aurora and Englewood. It also caused the second lightning-strike incident in two days in Douglas County. The day before, a woman in her fifties had been watching a Little League Veteran's Memorial baseball tournament game at Falcon Park in Highlands Ranch south of Denver. Umpires stopped the game as a storm approached, and spectators took refuge beneath tents and in cars. The woman, holding an umbrella, was standing under a tree when lightning hit nearby at about 4:20 P.M. The woman collapsed, and an ER nurse at the game named Pauline Parises rushed to her aid. "She said she couldn't feel her legs so we just held her neck straight and waited for the paramedics," Parises said. Bystanders kept the victim warm and dry until paramedics came and took her to the hospital, where she was treated for minor flash burns and nerve damage. The incident was a strong reminder that a tree or tent isn't adequate shelter in a lightning storm. The safest place is inside a building with electrical or plumbing service (because they're grounded) or in a vehicle.

On August 13, 2017, John Huisjen and his girlfriend were mountain biking on the East Fork Trail south of Colorado Highway 145 on the

Lightning often occurs along many paths at once, adding to its unpredictability and potential lethality. PHOTOGRAPH BY SHANE LEAR, COURTESY OF THE NATIONAL OCEANIC AND ATMOSPHERIC ADMINISTRATION.

Dolores Ranger District of the San Juan National Forest. Huisjen, twenty-four, was a 2015 graduate of Fort Lewis College in Durango. As they rode, a small but violent storm swept in, sending them and other nearby riders ducking for cover. Huisjen's girlfriend said she heard a loud crack, and she and Huisjen talked for a minute about how close the lightning must've been. Then, suddenly, Huisjen collapsed and stopped breathing. The girlfriend began giving CPR, but after five minutes she ran for help. She happened to find an off-duty Telluride emergency medical technician (EMT) who was also biking with a friend that day.

The EMT administered CPR, while his companion ran down the trail until he got cellphone coverage and called 9-1-1. The EMT hoped that first responders would be nearby with an automated external defibrillator (AED), to jump-start Huisjen's heart. Other bystanders assisted with CPR. Telluride deputies and search-and-rescue personnel hiked to the scene, but they could not revive Huisjen and he was pronounced dead. San Miguel County Sheriff Bill Masters praised the off-duty EMT, bystanders, and other responders, saying they did "everything they could for this young man."

Another lightning strike on Sunday, June 30, 2019, could have ended very badly for the people involved. That day, a party of eight climbers and a dog were enjoying the routes on Chicken Head Ranch, a granite outcrop in the Devil's Head area west of Castle Rock. Around 3 P.M., it started to rain, and the group huddled together under a rock wall. But lightning hit the wall near the climbers, knocking several to the ground.

In an interview afterward, climber Sydney Copeland said, "The girl behind me, I think she got struck. . . . She fell forward and was paralyzed pretty instantly." Copeland said she felt numbness and tingling and also had burns on one leg.

One of the less-injured climbers walked 1.5 miles to find phone service and called 9-1-1. There was an immediate multiagency response. The Douglas County Search and Rescue team, Jackson 105 Fire Protection District, Larkspur Fire Protection District, Castle Rock Fire Department, U.S. Forest Service rangers, and members of the Douglas County Sheriff's Department all participated in the rescue. All eight climbers suffered some degree of injury from the strike, but seven were able to walk out. The eighth, the woman mentioned by Copeland, was in critical condition and was carried out on a litter and transported to a hospital for treatment. Copeland said, "It was easily the scariest thing that will probably ever happen in my life."

On July 14, 2019, Peter Jornroth, a thirty-six-year-old Denver man, and his wife were taking a Sunday hike on the Bear Peak West Ridge Trail west of Boulder. They were only a quarter mile from the trailhead on Bison Road when lightning struck at about 1 P.M. Apparently, the bolt hit Peter and indirectly shocked his wife. Another hiker phoned for help while another passerby began CPR on Peter, who was unconscious and not breathing. Many agencies responded quickly, including personnel from the Boulder County Sheriff's Office, Rocky Mountain Fire Protection District, Rocky Mountain Rescue Group, Boulder County Parks and Open Space, City of Boulder Open Space and Mountain Parks, AMR Ambulance, and the Boulder Fire Department. A ranger from Boulder took over CPR and used a defibrillator, which reestablished Jornroth's pulse at the scene. He was evacuated by Air Live to a nearby hospital, where he later died. It is believed that the man took a direct hit to his upper body from the lightning. His wife suffered non-life-threatening injuries and was treated at the hospital.

While relatively few people are struck by lightning each year, the outcomes are often disastrous for victims and their friends and families. Few survive a direct hit, and even nearby strikes can be fatal when the current travels through the ground or another conductor. Survivors may suffer permanent injuries, including nerve damage, burn scars, memory and cognitive impairment, and loss of hearing. As these stories reveal, it's best to keep an eye on the sky and take shelter whenever lightning is a possibility.

SOURCES

Associated Press. "Woman and horse killed by lightning strike on popular riding trail." CBS News, May 8, 2017.

Byars, Mitchell. "Boulder County coroner identifies Denver man killed by lightning strike." Boulder *Daily Camera*, July 17, 2019.

Chavez, Jordan. "ER nurse in right place at right time when woman is injured by lightning strike." NBC 9 News, Denver, May 7, 2017.

Hickey, Chuck. "Denver man killed in Boulder County lightning strike identified." Fox 31 News, Denver, July 17, 2019.

Hodanish, Stephen J., Brandon J. Vogt, and Paul Wolyn. "Colorado Lightning Climatology." *Journal of Operational Meteorology*, National Weather Service, June 12, 2019.

"Lightning casualties by county." Colorado. 1980–2020. National Weather Service.

McKee, Spencer. "Lightning strike hits multiple people in Devil's Head Lookout area." *OutThere Colorado*, July 1, 2019.

Miller, Joshua Rhett. "Woman, decorated horse killed by lightning strike in Colorado." *New York Post*, May 8, 2017.

Mitchell, Chaffin. "Lightning strike injures 8 hikers at Devil's Head in Colorado." AccuWeather, July 8, 2019.

Mustin, Tom. "Man killed by lightning strike at golf course." CBS News 4, Denver, July 20, 2016.

"News Update: Mountain biker struck and killed by lightning." *Telluride Daily Planet*, August 14, 2017.

Osborne, Ryan. "Why lightning strikes this area more than anywhere else in Colorado." KOAA News 5, Colorado Springs, July 25, 2019.

Robles, Yesenia. "Man killed by Tuesday lightning strike in Arvada." *Denver Post*, July 20, 2016.

Westerkamp, Victor. "8 Hikers Hit by Lightning, 1 Critically Injured at Devil's Head in Colorado." NTD, July 3, 2019.

CHAPTER 7

TORNADOES

SAY "TORNADO" AND MOST PEOPLE THINK OF TEXAS, OKLAHOMA, Kansas, and Nebraska. Indeed, these states make up a loosely defined region known as Tornado Alley, where twisters occur more frequently than anywhere else in the country. But tornadoes also strike Colorado, particularly on the state's eastern plains. In fact, Weld County, northeast of Denver, sees more tornadoes than any other county in the United States. National Weather Service meteorologist Frank Cooper says that 270 tornadoes hit Weld County between 1950 and 2015. That's an average of four a year. Only one other county in the United States—Harris County, Texas—had more than 200 tornadoes during that same period. Researchers also say that the number of tornadoes in Colorado is on the rise, from a historical average of forty-seven per year to about sixty per year over the past decade.

Fortunately, most Weld County tornadoes aren't strong. Like the majority of Colorado's tornadoes, they are "land-spout" tornadoes, which means they form from the ground upward. These are weaker and shorter-lived than the supercell, top-down tornadoes common in Oklahoma and Texas. Supercell tornadoes are usually more dangerous, with higher wind speeds and an ability to grow into monsters with mile-wide funnels.

Tornado intensity is rated on the Enhanced Fujita, or EF, scale, which replaced the previous Fujita, or F, scale in 2007. Meteorologists assess the damage caused by a tornado to estimate the range of wind speed; the stronger the wind, the higher the EF number assigned to a given tornado. On the more intense end of the scale, an EF3 tornado has estimated wind speeds of 135 to 165 miles per hour, an EF4 166 to 200 miles per hour, and an EF5 more than 200 miles per hour.

A June 10, 2010, tornado hovers over Washington County, Colorado, near Last Chance, about seventy-five miles east of Denver. PHOTOGRAPH COURTESY OF THE NATIONAL OCEANIC AND ATMOSPHERIC ADMINISTRATION, NATIONAL SEVERE STORMS LABORATORY.

Many tornadoes touch down on open ground, doing relatively minor damage. But some hit populated areas, causing millions of dollars in property damage and injuring or killing people. The following stories reveal the power, lethality, and capriciousness of such storms.

HOLLY EF3, 2007

The small ranching and farming town of Holly sits just four miles from the border with Kansas in southeastern Colorado at an elevation of 3,392 feet, making it the lowest-elevation town in the state. Holly's 1,000 residents had no idea, on March 28, 2007, that their lives were about to forever change. That day, two powerful weather systems collided over the southern Great Plains, creating a near-continuous line of supercell thunderstorms from Lubbock, Texas, to Rapid City, South Dakota. The severe weather produced ninety-mile-per-hour, straight-line winds; softball-sized hail; and eighty confirmed tornadoes in six states. One of those tornadoes, an EF3, formed two miles south of Holly and then tore into town without warning just before 8 P.M.

"The weather was already bad," remembered Gustavo Puga, "but just like before, you never thought nothing of it, just bad weather." Puga, twenty-eight at the time, had just returned home with his family from a shopping trip to Lamar, the county seat, about thirty miles west. They dropped off their son, seven-year-old Gustavo Jr., at Puga's mother's house and then dashed into their home just down the street. They ate dinner, and then Puga heard a "loud, ugly noise." He grabbed his wife, Rosemary, and their three-year-old daughter, Noelia. "I just wrapped my arms around them," Puga recalled years later. "There was nothing else to do." The 600-foot-wide twister plowed directly into the home, sweeping it off its cinderblock foundation and tossing the Pugas into a cottonwood tree in their yard. Rosemary died the following day, leaving Gustavo and Noelia to recover from cuts, bruises, and fearful memories.

Another local woman, Dolores Burns, seventy-eight, passed away about a month later from injuries suffered in the storm. Eleven more people were injured that night, and the twister destroyed 43 homes and damaged 137 more as it ripped a two-mile path through town. It stayed on the ground for half an hour and cut a swath twenty-eight miles north through farmland before dissipating south of Towner. In Colorado, such severe tornadoes are rare in March, and the Holly funnel marks the earliest on record of an EF2 or stronger.

Since that violent night in 2007, about 200 fewer people call Holly home, but the community has rebounded in other ways: new homes, a rejuvenated Main Street that includes a new grocery store, and a new junior high/high school, home of the Wildcats. And despite the vivid memories—or perhaps because of them—Gustavo Puga still calls Holly home.

COLORADO'S DEADLIEST TWISTER, 1924

Thurman isn't a town so much as a couple of farm homes and outbuildings along a gravel road 100 miles east of Denver in a sea of crop fields. The vast sky arcs overhead and completes a perfect dome where it meets the distant, flat horizon in a seamless, 360-degree circle. In 1924, Thurman was slightly more developed, boasting a few shops, a church, and a school. Farmhouses dotted the surrounding plains. At 1 P.M. on Sunday, August 10, 1924, the sky turned dark, and an angry funnel touched the ground southwest of Thurman. The twister chewed a northeasterly path and dealt Thurman a direct blow, razing most of the buildings in town. Then it continued rumbling to the northeast.

A few miles from Thurman, Henry Kuhns and his family were hosting dinner guests after a midday church service: Joe Ioder and his wife and children, the Reverend Amos Burkey and his wife, and a man named Fred Garrett. The tornado ran smack into the Kuhns home and also demolished a chicken coop, barn, and two automobiles in the yard. Five of the people in the home were injured and ten killed, including four of the Ioder children, two of the Kuhns children and Mrs. Kuhns, Fred Garrett, and the Reverend Burkey.

Researchers later estimated that the tornado was a half mile wide and remained in contact with the ground for at least eight miles. The degree of damage suggested that this may have been an EF4 tornado with winds in excess of 165 miles per hour. It remains the deadliest tornado to ever hit Colorado.

WINDSOR EF3, 2008

Thursday, May 22, 2008, started out with clear, sunny skies along the Front Range. But as the day went on, warm, dry air to the south bumped into a cool, wet front to the north, and winds built aloft coming out of the southeast. The National Weather Service issued a watch for storms forming along the Front Range. A few hours later, that possibility became a reality. A supercell thunderstorm developed near Denver International Airport and began tracking north. It seemed to be headed straight toward Greeley. Then, as the storm passed east of Platteville and approached U.S. Highway 85, it spawned a tornado that veered slightly northwest. Instead of Greeley, it now had Windsor in its sights.

The funnel formed a three-quarter-mile-wide wedge that contained not just one vortex but up to seven tornadoes at once, with winds in excess of 165 miles per hour. It scattered cars and toppled semi-trailers along U.S.

The Windsor tornado, shown here west of Greeley, formed a wide wedge composed of multiple vortices. PHOTOGRAPH COURTESY OF THE NATIONAL WEATHER SERVICE.

Highway 85 near Gilcrest, then crossed the South Platte River and roared just east of Milliken. The massive wedge struck a dairy farm about a half mile from Missile Site Park west of Greeley, shredding a barn and littering a road with about seventy dead cows and calves.

Oscar "Mike" Manchester, a fifty-two-year-old military veteran, was camped at Missile Site Park in his trailer. A witness said that the tornado "picked up [the trailer] and smashed it to the ground. It ripped the whole top of it off. It ripped the carpet right off the floor," killing Manchester in the process.

Then, at 11:30 A.M., churning along at thirty miles per hour, the EF3 vortex steamrolled into the southeast side of Windsor with almost no warning. Hail pelted the town and people ran for shelter. David Parsons, a retired newspaperman, took cover in the Windsor *Beacon* newsroom on Main Street. The building had originally been a bank and still had a small vault. As the front doors blew open and office supplies swirled in the turbulence, Parsons and a reporter huddled in the vault.

After the vortex passed, Parsons drove through town, observing the damage. Homes were leveled, cars mangled, and trees stripped bare and uprooted. Parsons saw one man walking with his basset hound; when they turned a corner, the man discovered his house was gone. A metal garage was torn from its foundations and dropped in a twisted heap in a field seventy yards away. One man told Parsons he had clung to his kitchen sink while the back part of his home flew off into the sky. Down the street, the wooden slats from a fence were embedded like spears in the siding of a house.

Damage in Windsor was severe. PHOTOGRAPH COURTESY OF THE NATIONAL WEATHER SERVICE.

The tornado's destruction was random. Windsor resident Liz Meyer said she heard thunder, hail, and rain and rushed with her dog into her basement. When she came upstairs again, she saw that her house had escaped damage but a sixty-foot tree from two blocks away had been uprooted and dumped in the street out front. The storm took down many power lines, cutting electricity to 60,000 customers. The wind even toppled tombstones at a local cemetery.

Jolene Schneider, spokeswoman for the Windsor Fire Department, told reporters, "We have every type of injury, broken bones, cuts, bruises, from everything from falling trees to broken glass hitting them. The only thing we are trying to figure out now is how many and how severe." A daycare center was badly damaged, but the children waited out part of the

Some homes in Windsor suffered catastrophic damage. PHOTOGRAPH COURTESY OF THE NATIONAL WEATHER SERVICE.

storm and then took shelter in a nearby bank. Schools in the affected areas, most of which were celebrating the final day of classes, were put on lockdown until the storm passed, and parents later picked up their children.

No warning sirens sounded that afternoon in Windsor, because the town did not have them and still doesn't today. In fact, few Front Range communities do. Such warning systems are regarded by some as "dinosaurs" in weather technology. They're expensive to install and maintain, and many people do not want pole-mounted sirens close to their homes. Instead, many towns now send alerts by phone text, email, television, and radio. Mike Gavin, emergency manager for Fort Collins, said, "The current systems we use are very rapid, and instead of just hearing a noise that says, 'Houston we have a problem,' it gives you information as to what the problem is and what immediate action you have to take to save lives and property."

Governor Bill Ritter declared a state of emergency and called out the National Guard. The Red Cross set up a shelter in Windsor, and 500 people also sheltered at the Budweiser Event Center and Fairgrounds in Larimer County.

While Windsor was hardest hit that day, tornadoes also caused damage near Dacono and in Greeley, where the State Farm Insurance regional headquarters took a direct hit. Regionwide, seventy-eight people were injured

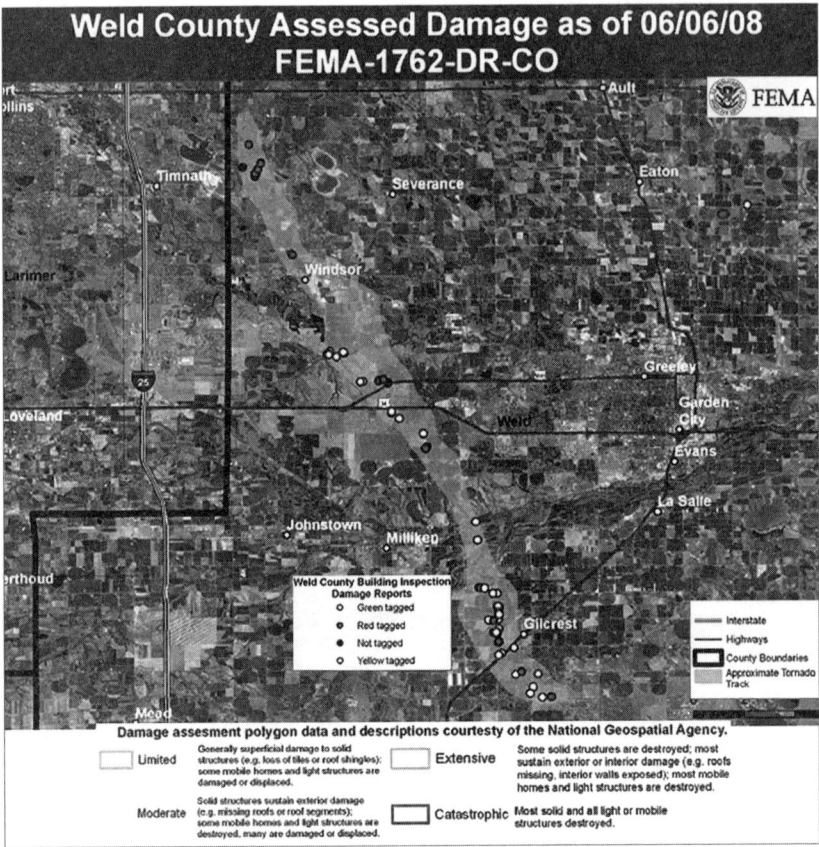

Weld County Assessed Damage as of 06/06/08
FEMA-1762-DR-CO

Weld County Building Inspection Damage Reports
- ○ Green tagged
- ● Red tagged
- ● Not tagged
- ○ Yellow tagged

- Interstate
- Highways
- County Boundaries
- Approximate Tornado Track

Damage assessment polygon data and descriptions courtesy of the National Geospatial Agency.

Limited Generally superficial damage to solid structures (e.g. loss of tiles or roof shingles); some mobile homes and light structures are damaged or displaced.

Moderate Solid structures sustain exterior damage (e.g. missing roofs or roof segments); some mobile homes and light structures are destroyed, many are damaged or displaced.

Extensive Some solid structures are destroyed; most sustain exterior or interior damage (e.g. roofs missing, interior walls exposed); most mobile homes and light structures are destroyed.

Catastrophic Most solid and all light or mobile structures destroyed.

The Windsor twister plowed a northwesterly path, unusual for tornadoes, leaving a wide swatch of destruction. IMAGE COURTESY OF THE FEDERAL EMERGENCY MANAGEMENT ADMINISTRATION AND NATIONAL WEATHER SERVICE.

that day, and the Federal Emergency Management Agency estimated that 850 homes were damaged, 300 of them severely or completely. Insured damages totaled $147 million, and the Poudre Valley utility reported $1 million in damage to transmission lines, making this the most costly tornado in Colorado history.

SOURCES
Marmaduke, Jacy. "Forget Tornado Alley: Weld County is No. 1 for twisters." *Coloradoan*, June 2, 2016.

Holly EF3, 2007
Aguilera, Elizabeth. "Holly tornado: total destruction." *Denver Post*, March 29, 2007.

Mestas, Anthony. "10 years after the storm: Community comes together to breathe new life, hope into Holly." *Pueblo Chieftain*, March 25, 2017.

Mestas, Anthony. "Holly tornado: Thoughts of tragic night linger." *Pueblo Chieftain*, March 25, 2017.

Simpson, Kevin. "Tornado takes life of mom flung into tree." *Denver Post*, March 29, 2007.

Colorado's Deadliest Twister, 1924

"Home razed, 15 victims taken in wind storm." *Nevada State Journal*, August 11, 1924.

"Thurman, Colorado tornado of 1924." National Weather Service, www.weather.gov/bou/1924ThurmanTornado.

Windsor EF2, 2008

Associated Press. "Tornado rips through N. Colorado; 1 killed." *Los Angeles Times*, May 22, 2008.

Lindsey, Daniel T., Steven D. Miller, Jeff Braun, and Dan Bikos. "An Analysis of the 22 May 2008 Windsor, Colorado, Tornado." American Meteorological Society 24th Conference on Severe Local Storms, October 27, 2008.

Marmaduke, Jacy. "Why Fort Collins doesn't have tornado sirens." *Coloradoan*, May 9, 2017.

"May 22, 2008 Windsor Tornado." National Weather Service, Denver/Boulder Weather Forecast Office.

Nicholson, Kieran. "Mile-wide tornado hits Windsor, Weld County." *Denver Post*, May 22, 2008.

Simpson, Kevin. "Tornado plows through Greeley, Windsor; one dead." *Denver Post*, May 23, 2008.

CHAPTER 8

BLIZZARDS AND AVALANCHES

COLORADO SITS AT A CROSSROADS OF WEATHER PATTERNS THAT CARRY moisture from the Pacific Ocean and Gulf of Mexico and cold air down from Canada. So it's no surprise that snowstorms and blizzards occasionally slam the state. Coloradoans were mostly spared from the brutal Schoolhouse, or Children's, Blizzard of January 1888, which killed 235 people, including many children, in Nebraska, Kansas, Wyoming, the Dakotas, and Minnesota. But other winter storms have brought parts of the Centennial State to a standstill.

Mountain towns and ski resorts are famed for heavy snowfalls, but the Front Range actually experiences worse storms. In fact, Silver Lake, in the Front Range west of Boulder, holds the record for the highest twenty-four-hour snowfall total in the Lower 48 states—an astonishing 75.8 inches on April 14–15, 1921. According to the Colorado Climate Center, that same storm piled a total of 95 inches over 32.5 hours at Silver Lake. Denver saw only 10 inches from the storm, but fifty-mile-per-hour winds whipped the snow into seven-foot drifts across the city.

Big snowstorms hit Denver with some regularity. In early November 1946, 30.4 inches fell on the city over seventy hours, bringing streetcars and traffic to a halt. A Christmas Eve storm in 1982 dropped 23.2 inches on Denver, and high winds drifted snow completely over cars, livestock, and even homes. The region saw 21.9 inches of snow in October 1997, stranding more than 4,000 passengers at the then-new Denver International Airport.

Colorado storms also dump snow in the mountains, supplying all the ingredients needed to create deadly avalanches: copious snow, steep slopes, and homes and businesses—sometimes whole towns—located near or within avalanche paths. Given the number of people who live and recreate today in the mountains, it's surprising that most of the state's deadliest avalanches occurred in the nineteenth and early twentieth centuries. All of those slides hit mining camps, and they no doubt served as potent cautionary tales as people eventually learned to avoid avalanche zones when siting towns.

In his research paper, "A History of Colorado Avalanche Accidents," avalanche expert Dale Atkins reported that the first documented avalanche fatality in Colorado occurred on March 6, 1861, when a prospector was buried by a snowslide in the Hall Valley, near the headwaters of the North Fork of the South Platte River. (Another lethal slide would strike in the same vicinity sixteen years later; see below.) From that first death in 1861 through 2006 when he presented his paper, Atkins had confirmed 409 fatal avalanches in Colorado that claimed a total of 693 lives. Within the entire United States, about 100,000 avalanches occur each year, killing an annual average of twenty people. Most of these slides occur in Colorado, Idaho, Montana, Nevada, Utah, and Wyoming, and today most of the victims are skiers and snowmobilers.

Let's dig into two major blizzards and then venture into a series of avalanche stories.

DECEMBER BLIZZARD, 1913

The big daddy of Colorado blizzards hit back in December 1913. The storm dropped copious amounts of snow across a wide swath of the state. A total of 45.7 inches of snow fell on Denver, the largest snowfall from a single storm in the city's history and a record that still stands today. A disaster? Perhaps not in terms of lives lost, but the damage, destruction, and disruption were significant and widespread, paralyzing Denver for days.

Snow began falling on December 1 in the Denver metro area and continued for four days. The city came to a standstill. As the *Denver Post*

The 1913 blizzard buried Denver homes and streets. PHOTOGRAPH DONATED BY THE *ROCKY MOUNTAIN NEWS*, COURTESY OF THE DENVER PUBLIC LIBRARY, RMN-032-7945.

front page bleated, "No Trains . . . No Schools . . . No Noises, No Taxis, No Mails, No Deliveries, No Funerals."

As with subsequent blizzards to hit the region, the 1913 storm stemmed from a combination of factors. A low-pressure weather system slid in from the Four Corners region and was held over Colorado by a high-pressure system to the north. This pumped moisture from the Gulf of Mexico onto the eastern plains. A phenomenon that meteorologists call "upslope flow" drew that moisture toward the Front Range. As the air lifted over the rising terrain, it cooled and dropped its load of moisture. Temperatures hovered at freezing, so the snow that fell was wet and heavy.

The depth and weight of the falling snow soon became deadly. Many flat-roofed buildings caved in, and even some pitched roofs couldn't bear the strain. At the Antlers Hotel near Colorado Springs, the roof of the stables collapsed, killing eleven of the twenty-six horses kept there.

Most homes and businesses in Denver at that time relied on coal for heat. Because transportation had been knocked out, coal deliveries stopped. This created a real hardship for those who had a limited supply of coal on hand. The *Denver Post* building had a large stockpile of coal, so during the blizzard the newspaper sold and even gave away some of its supply to needy families.

The publishers also sent wagonloads of coal to St. Clara Orphanage, north of Sloan's Lake. When the wagons got stuck near a circus that was camped and waiting out the storm, the drivers enlisted the help of elephants to free the wagons so they could complete their delivery.

Transportation of all kinds was totally disrupted. By the afternoon of December 1, road conditions were already a mess, and by that evening many cars, which had only recently become popular in Denver, were so badly blocked that they were abandoned. Many people had no way of getting home from work, and hotels and boardinghouses quickly filled. Some people simply stayed in their workplaces, while others found shelter in police stations. A small crowd spent the night in the city auditorium.

Some streetcars continued to run, but by the fourth day, all 200 miles of Denver's electric-streetcar system was shut down, and 210 streetcars were marooned throughout the city. Students from the Colorado School of Mines dug nonstop for three days to free passengers stuck in streetcars.

The *Denver Post* commented, "The only means of transportation was a sturdy pair of legs." Faced with knee-deep snow on sidewalks, Denver Mayor James M. Perkins called on all able-bodied citizens to help shovel snow. By the fifth day of the storm, the streetcar system had hired 4,000 men to clear its routes.

There was so much snow that the City of Denver finally hired men at $2.50 a day to shovel sidewalks. This helped many people who were losing wages because they couldn't get to their regular jobs.

Horse and mule trains and wagons were pressed into use to haul the snow away. The biggest problem facing Denver was where to put it all. Any open space or park became a magnet, attracting anyone who needed to dump loads of snow. This problem continued for many days after the storm. Sometimes only one lane down the middle of a street was open, and men worked for days to clear the entire street.

Some of the snow was taken down 16th Street toward Broadway and then dumped into Cherry Creek. The open space near the state Capitol, now Civic Center Park, was filled with loads of snow brought in by horse- and mule-drawn wagons. The piles were so deep, they didn't completely melt until summer.

Since Denver was at a standstill, children of all ages enjoyed a "snow day," here sledding on Eighth Avenue. PHOTOGRAPH DONATED BY THE *ROCKY MOUNTAIN NEWS*, COURTESY OF THE DENVER PUBLIC LIBRARY, RMN-032-7947.

Since schools and streets were closed, people made the most of the unexpected snow vacation. Children got out their sleds. In the Capitol Hill area, adults organized ski teams. Karl Howelsen, a ski salesman from Norway, made the most of the blizzard. He gave free ski lessons to anyone interested, splitting his time between Denver and Routt County. He helped organize the first winter carnival in Steamboat Springs. He is credited today with starting the Colorado ski industry.

As challenging as the snow was in Denver, the situation was even worse in mountain towns to the west. Telegraph wires fell, so many communities were completely out of touch with the rest of the world. Up to sixty inches of snow fell in Central City and fifty-three inches in Estes Park. Georgetown was hardest hit, receiving eighty-six inches. Struggling under more than seven feet of snow and cut off from outside news sources, the Georgetown newspaper printed a December 6 edition that was only four pages long, and two of those pages were completely blank.

Cripple Creek saw forty inches of snow, and drifts were ten to twenty feet deep. A Midland Terminal Railway passenger train got stuck in the snow on Victor Pass just outside Goldfield. Twenty-five passengers had to fight their way through deep snow to reach the safety of town. It took many days to dig out the train tracks using an eleven-foot-tall rotary snowplow. Throughout the state, at least twenty trains were stuck on the tracks and had to be dug out.

Above Woodland Park, the Gayler Homestead on Bald Mountain received twenty *feet* of snow. Even the eastern plains saw heavy snow and fierce winds. Farmhouses, barns, and roads were blanketed with deep snow. Although farmers did all they could to help their animals, it is estimated that thousands of cattle died. Along the Wyoming border, there were reports of snowdrifts thirty to fifty feet high. Weeks went by before transportation routes to these towns could be reestablished. Other nearby cities also received huge quantities of snow. Boulder had 43 inches, Fort Collins 33.5, and Colorado Springs 24.4 inches.

Records of fatalities and injuries from this storm are spotty, but some historians place the death toll at thirty-four. Some people died when their roofs collapsed, while others succumbed to exposure. With plenty of hardship to go around, some people rose to the occasion with acts of kindness. In Colorado Springs, a Santa Fe Railroad crew shoveled coal from their tenders to the ground beside the tracks for locals to use to heat their homes. And north of the Springs, generous souls brought a supply of food by mule train for the 200 residents of the Modern Woodmen Tuberculosis Sanitarium.

By December 10, Denver had dug out from the worst of the snow. Schools were in session again, and coal and grocery deliveries were returning to normal. The following year, farmers on the plains reaped a "golden harvest" thanks to the extra moisture stored in the soil. And city officials throughout the region enacted new design standards requiring buildings and roofs to withstand greater loads.

ST. PATRICK'S DAY BLIZZARD, 2003

The second-strongest blizzard to hit Denver came almost exactly ninety years later on St. Patrick's Day in 2003. The storm started on Monday,

March 17, with rain, thunderstorms, and even a tornado (which did no damage) on the eastern plains. Then heavy snow began falling, from Cheyenne, Wyoming, to the Denver metro area. Up and down the Front Range, snow fell at a rate of 0.5 to 1 inch per hour and continued for three days. Denver Mayor Wellington E. Webb said, "It's a record breaker, a backbreaker, and a roof breaker."

At times, the wind gusted over forty miles per hour, creating huge drifts. The heavy spring snow ripped a hole in the tentlike roof of Denver International Airport. The airport closed, and several thousand passengers were stranded. Just sixty miles to the southeast, Colorado Springs Municipal Airport received only three inches of snow and remained open.

Denver schools closed, as did those in Boulder and Jefferson Counties, and most remained closed for a week. Many city and state government offices also closed. By the third day of the storm, many businesses were closed because employees could not get to work. But customers were scarce, too. Although snowplow drivers worked twelve-hour shifts, most neighborhood streets remained unplowed because the snow was higher than the plow blade, and drivers couldn't see where to drive. Many neighborhood streets remained impassable until Saturday, March 23.

Strong winds drifted heavy snow into car-burying piles during the St. Patrick's Day blizzard of 2003.
PHOTOGRAPH COURTESY OF THE NATIONAL OCEANIC AND ATMOSPHERIC ADMINISTRATION.

Claims Quarterly reported that, for the first quarter of 2003, Colorado had the highest insured loss in the whole country, and the bulk of this loss was due to the blizzard.

Temperatures throughout the storm were near freezing, so the snow was especially wet and heavy. At least 110 roofs of businesses and homes collapsed, many on older buildings that had been built to hold only 10 to 20 pounds per square foot. Modern building codes in Denver require roofs to be capable of holding 25 to 30 pounds per square foot. But this snow was so wet that a three-foot accumulation would weigh 36.5 pounds per square foot. In spite of the many roofs that collapsed, especially on flat-roofed commercial buildings in Denver and Boulder, there were few injuries and no deaths. This was probably due to the fact that most of these businesses had closed and were unoccupied.

Two people in Aurora died during the storm due to heart attacks while shoveling snow. The snow was also blamed for one traffic death in Colorado and two in Wyoming. In Denver, a snowmobiler helping a stranded family was killed in an accident.

About 135,000 people lost power during the storm, some for several days. Many highways were impassable. Interstate 70 was closed but then reopened Thursday, March 20, from Denver to the Kansas border after 1,500 plows worked to clear it. Fifty-six miles of I-70 remained closed in the mountains west of Denver, as well as parts of I-25 and I-80 in Wyoming. More than 2,500 motorists were stranded. Some were rescued by the National Guard, and many took refuge in Red Cross shelters.

When the storm ended, 31.8 inches of snow had fallen in Denver. Boulder received 22.5 inches, Fort Collins 28 inches, Golden 50 inches, and Evergreen, in the foothills west of Denver, got 73 inches.

It's not often that a snowstorm closes a ski resort, but the 2003 storm did just that. Winter Park Ski Resort received 120 inches of snow. Vail reported 58 inches, and Breckenridge saw 74 inches. The blizzard caused many avalanches in the mountains and foothills. One of these swept past the slopes of Nederland's Eldora Mountain Ski Resort. All the runs were closed, and about 300 skiers were trapped in the lodge for two nights. They looked out on beautiful, fresh snow that was too dangerous to ski on, and they slept on hard floors.

The blizzard was good news in one respect. Colorado had been experiencing a drought for the previous four years. The mountain snowpack, which is needed to fill lakes and reservoirs, had been only 85 percent of normal. So the blizzard was a blessing to farmers whose crops would be irrigated by the welcome shot of water. It also promised fewer devastating forest fires the following summer.

THE FIRST HALL VALLEY AVALANCHE, 1877

One of the first mass-casualty avalanches in Colorado occurred in the Hall Valley on January 7, 1877, just a few miles southeast of today's Keystone Resort ski area. The slide hit early in the morning, demolishing a cluster of cabins near the Whale Mine and catching miners asleep in their bunks. One miner who survived, George Cardier, said the impact was so forceful it knocked his boots and socks off his feet. The slide killed eight people, including a family of four.

WOODSTOCK AVALANCHE, 1884

On March 10, 1884, without warning, a massive slide hit the small settlement of Woodstock in Gunnison County. Founded in 1881 on a short spur of the Denver, South Park & Pacific Railroad, Woodstock sat at the base of 12,757-foot Mount Chapman and consisted of a boardinghouse, telegraph office, saloon, train depot, water tank, and a few homes and outbuildings. All told, about thirty people lived there.

A widow, Marcella Doyle, managed the boardinghouse, Delmonica's, and lived there with her six children, who ranged in age from ten to twenty-three. Most of the boarders were employees of the railroad. Mrs. Doyle's two oldest sons also worked for the railroad. Her younger children and a woman named Cecilia Dillon helped with chores. Freight agents and miners came and went, staying either at Delmonica's or in one of the shacks around town.

On the evening of March 10, in addition to the eight people at Delmonica's, the town's population included the telegraph operator; station manager J. S. Brown; saloon owner James Mulholland; bartender Joseph Gerazo; section boss Mike Shea; and railroad workers Jim Tracy, George Alexander, Peter Walpole, and Joe Royegno. A miner named Jasper Caswell and three visitors were also in town. The three visitors boarded the train at 6:05 P.M.

The Denver, South Park & Pacific train left Woodstock and was slowly climbing three miles of snowy track to the Alpine Tunnel when a 125-foot-wide swath of snow broke loose and came hurtling down the southwest face of Mount Chapman. From his window seat on the train, Eugene A. Teats watched the slide barrel down the slope. "The crashing and roaring was like the tearing away of a mountain," Teats said, and indeed it was, as the avalanche scoured rocks and trees as it plowed downhill. The blast of snow and debris smashed into the train station, boardinghouse, and saloon. It destroyed or severely damaged every building in town and swept everything into the gully below. Even the railroad tracks were ripped from the ground and carried far down the mountain.

One man who was in the boardinghouse at the time of the avalanche managed to free himself from the wreckage. After trying to help others, he ran almost two miles to the keeper of the Midway water tank to tell what had happened. The man there skied to the town of Pitkin to get help. It took many hours

The avalanche demolished this wood frame house in Woodstock.
PHOTOGRAPH COURTESY OF THE DENVER PUBLIC LIBRARY, SPECIAL COLLECTIONS, Z-2768.

for rescue teams to arrive, both from the Denver side and from Pitkin. The temperature was about 40 degrees below zero, so it was remarkable that rescuers discovered Marcella Doyle and Cecilia Dillon alive after being buried for twelve and fifteen hours, respectively. Two men were also found alive, but the death toll numbered thirteen people, including all six of the Doyle children: Andrew, Christopher, Katy, Maggie, Martin, and a daughter also named Marcella.

As Mrs. Doyle pointed out in a lawsuit after the tragedy, Woodstock had been built directly in an avalanche path. She sued for $50,000, but the case was dismissed. The court record of January 23, 1893, stated, "The Plaintiff's evidence failed wholly to show that there was any special and secret danger from snow slides which was known only to the railway company, and which could not have been ascertained by the plaintiff." Later, however, the camp of Tunnel Gulch was built about one-half mile from Woodstock's former site and out of any avalanche paths. This was considered a tacit admission that the site for Woodstock had been poorly chosen. Some speculated that the train itself may have triggered the avalanche. Woodstock was never rebuilt and is now a ghost town with just a few remnant building foundations. The 1884 incident there remains the deadliest single avalanche in Colorado's history.

HOMESTAKE MINE SLIDE, 1885

Barely less than a year later, on February 22, 1885, an avalanche fifteen miles north of Leadville typified the snowslide disasters of Colorado's mining era. Mine owners and operators tended to situate housing as close to the mine workings as possible. They usually tried to avoid building in obvious slide paths, but the risks were not always clear. Sometimes, many years would pass between avalanches, and trees would grow in the old slide paths, hiding evidence of potential danger. In other cases, an unusually large avalanche would extend beyond any previous runout zone, sometimes even charging up an opposite slope that had seemed well out of danger.

In this instance, heavy snowfall over thirteen consecutive days created conditions ripe for a larger-than-expected avalanche. The slide hit near the

Homestake Mine, demolishing a supply cabin and a bunkhouse, killing ten of the eleven men inside. According to a brief article in *The New York Times*, rescuers could not reach the site for two weeks due to deep, soft snow. When they finally trekked in on snowshoes, they had to dig down through deep snow just to find the buildings. Inside the bunkhouse, they found one man frozen standing up, "head thrown forward, as if listening, the whole position indicating apprehension." Another knelt by a bunk, as if praying. A few of the men were crushed by fallen timbers, but it was presumed that most suffocated to death.

Men pause from digging out the cabin buried by the avalanche at the Homestake Mine. PHOTOGRAPH COURTESY OF THE DENVER PUBLIC LIBRARY, SPECIAL COLLECTIONS,x-60006.

The dead included prospectors from England, Nova Scotia, Iowa, and California. There were two sets of brothers: Martin and Sylvester Borden, and Horace and Joseph Matthews. In an odd coincidence, also among the dead were two men named John Burns.

SILVER PLUME AND THE BIG SNOW WINTER, 1898–1899

The town of Silver Plume arose after a rich strike of gold was made at the Griffith Mine near Georgetown. This was the only large amount of gold discovered locally, but in the 1860s there were many silver strikes, and Silver Plume was incorporated in 1880. Nearby, several famous mines yielded their precious ores: the Argentine, Burleigh, Pelican, and 7:30 (so named because the morning shift started a generous hour later than at other mines). More than $100 million worth of silver came out of the Silver Plume district.

The town sat on the north bank of Clear Creek at the feet of Sherman and Republican Mountains. Homes and businesses lined the bench above the creek, and mine openings and tunnels dotted the steep, rocky slopes above. In 1884, a fire swept through town, destroying most of the commercial district, but silver output remained strong, so businesses rebuilt. By the early 1890s, Silver Plume's population had grown to more than 2,000—a multicultural mix of people from several European countries, the East Coast, and the Midwest.

The town of Silver Plume sits at the base of the steep, rocky slopes of Sherman and Republican Mountains. PHOTOGRAPH COURTESY OF THE LIBRARY OF CONGRESS, LC-USZ62-110842.

But trouble arrived during the winter of 1898–1899 in the form of more snow than anyone imagined possible. In Breckenridge, just twenty-three miles southwest as the crow flies, it snowed for seventy-nine days straight, from November 27, 1898, to February 20, 1899. And it wasn't just flurries—on November 28, residents woke up to five feet of fresh powder. The snow kept coming. By February 5, trains could no longer get to towns in Summit County; service didn't resume until the last week of April. Food supplies ran low, and fresh dairy products, eggs, and vegetables were nonexistent. Worst of all, saloons ran out of whiskey! The season became known as the Big Snow Winter, and it remains the snowiest on record in Colorado. Single-story cabins were completely buried. A mail carrier on snowshoes crossing Boreas Pass could not find the railroad station house until he stumbled on smoke coming from a chimney six inches below the snow surface. He then found steps cut into the snow that led twenty feet down to the door. Even in towns, the snow reached the eaves of homes, and access to hotels was often through second-story windows.

The results for Silver Plume were tragic, though perhaps not unpredictable. At 8 A.M. on Sunday, February 12, the huge load of snow on Sherman Mountain broke loose and began falling toward Silver Plume. The slide started in Carry City Gulch (labeled as Corry City Gulch on era maps) and roared over the Pelican Mine's tunnel house, sweeping with it the mine dumps and several buildings. As this slide reached Cherokee Gulch, the snow in Swallow Hen Gulch on the opposite flank broke away, and the two enormous slides merged as they careened down Cherokee Gulch toward town.

Just above Silver Plume, a settlement of about 200 Italian miners lived in a scattering of small cabins, several of which were directly in the path of the avalanche. Most of the trees in this area had been cut for fuel, to build cabins, and for use in the mines, so nothing impeded the onrushing snowslide. It barreled into the settlement, instantly crushing a handful of cabins and carrying the debris downhill along with huge boulders. Then, just before downtown Silver Plume, a sharp bend in the gulch slowed and stopped the avalanche.

Some of the slide did reach into the east side of town as far as the playground of the two-story, brick schoolhouse that had been built just four

The avalanche filled this building at the 7:30 Mine with hard-packed snow. PHOTOGRAPH COURTESY OF THE DENVER PUBLIC LIBRARY, SPECIAL COLLECTIONS, X-17693.

years earlier. No children were present—it was a Sunday morning—and amazingly, no one in town was injured by the slide.

Word quickly spread in Silver Plume that the avalanche had struck miners' cabins, and at first it was feared that fifty or sixty people might have been killed. Men from Silver Plume and Georgetown scrambled to the site, helped survivors, and dug out the bodies of victims. The dead were carried out on makeshift sleds hauled by teams of men, because horses couldn't manage the deep snow on the road. When people in town saw men dragging something across the slope above, they knew another body had been found.

The rescuers faced tremendous obstacles. The snow and debris at the foot of the gulch was seventy-five feet deep, and the demolished cabins were scattered over a large area. Digging in the hard-packed slide was nearly as challenging as digging in the mines. Eventually, crews recovered the bodies of six miners, a miner's wife, and two children ages five and two. Three men were found alive but with serious injuries, including broken bones, bruises, and head and internal injuries.

The Knights of Pythias Hall at the end of town was used as a temporary morgue. All of the bodies were recovered the day of the avalanche except for one, that of Domenico Destefane, whose wife, Caterina, and two children, Giovanni and Maria, were among the dead. Domenico's body remained missing until the snow melted several months later.

The funerals took place on the following Tuesday. Gone were Mrs. Destefane and her two children, as well as Girolamo Guenzi, Battista Bietto, Enrico Noaria, and brothers Giuseppe, Pietro, and Giovanni Tondini. Delegations of miners from Central City, Black Hawk, and Georgetown came to pay their respects. The caskets, black for the adults and white for the two children, were taken from the morgue by a draped wagon to the opera house, which was filled with mourners. All were buried side by side in one plot, with a space left for Domenico Destefane next to his wife and children.

Adding to the gloom, a 100-foot-tall snowdrift still clung to Sherman Mountain above the fracture face of the avalanche. Many townsfolk expected that the worst was yet to come. Unfortunately, just ten days later, on February 22, another slide charged down Brown Gulch just west of town. It hit the 7:30 Mine, destroying mine buildings, killing three men, and injuring four.

Eventually, a tall, granite column was erected near the Italians' grave in the Silver Plume cemetery. Its inscription reads, "Sacred to the memory of the ten Italians, victims of an avalanche. February 12, 1899. Erected by the public."

LIBERTY BELL MINE AVALANCHES, 1902

Heavy snowfall also accounted for a series of three short but deadly avalanches on February 28, 1902, at the Liberty Bell Mine above Telluride. A foot of fresh snow had fallen the day prior, and more accumulated overnight. The first slide struck at 7:30 A.M., shortly after the day shift had gone into the mine to start work. The normally dangerous interior of the mine proved to be safer at that moment than anywhere aboveground.

A mule packer, L. M. Umsted, was saddling his animals in the stables when the building began to rattle and shake. Then it went dark, as though night had fallen. As it grew light again, Umsted peeked outside and saw tram buckets rolling downhill and the tram cable swinging loose. The boardinghouse no longer stood in its familiar place, and one corner of a new bunkhouse (where the day shift had slept the night away) was demolished. Also gone were the tram house and the building housing the

The Liberty Bell Mine perched precariously on the steep slopes of Greenback Mountain, a spur below 13,581-foot Mount Emma. PHOTOGRAPH COURTESY OF THE DENVER PUBLIC LIBRARY, SPECIAL COLLECTIONS, x-62359.

ore crusher. Thankfully, the slide missed an old bunkhouse where the sixty-man night crew was snoring away.

The slide took down the telephone lines, so it was an hour before a survivor reached town and rallied a rescue party. Their work was slowed by continued heavy snowfall. Then, just after noon, a second slide came down the path of the first, burying some of the rescuers. Again a call for help went down to town, and again men rushed up the hill. But the weather deteriorated, and the men feared the mountain would release more walls of snow. As the rescuers abandoned their search and headed back to town, a third slide caught a small party of men near the tram line, killing three.

By 4:15 P.M., the mine manager somberly gave the list of dead and injured to the editor of the *Daily Journal* in Telluride. Seven men had died in the first slide, including two recent graduates of the state School of Mines who were working only to gain a little hands-on experience before taking jobs in mine management. The second slide had killed two rescuers, and the third had killed a miner, a head mechanic, and a surveyor. In total, twelve men died and eight more lay in the hospital with broken bones and internal injuries.

It would be four months before the mine could resume operations. Besides rebuilding the tramway, bunkhouse, and other buildings, workers also erected a V-shaped timber crib filled with rock to divert future avalanches. In 1906, the crib did its job, redirecting a slide away from structures and people.

SHENANDOAH-DIVES SLIDE, 1906

One of the deadliest avalanches in state history occurred in March 1906 at the Shenandoah Mine near Silverton. Details of the event vary according to which account you read. Some say it happened on March 17, others on March 19. Some say the slide hit a boardinghouse while miners were eating dinner; others insist that the miners had run out of food and were walking to Silverton to avoid starvation. In the latter version, one miner stumbled on a precarious section of trail and set off the slide. A note in the March 20,

The slopes surrounding the Shenandoah-Dives Mine, shown here circa 1910, were clearly avalanche prone. PHOTOGRAPH COURTESY OF THE DENVER PUBLIC LIBRARY, SPECIAL COLLECTIONS, X-62231.

1906, *Arizona Journal-Miner* mentioned both scenarios without favoring one or the other. Such is the fuzzy line of history after more than a century.

We do know that the Shenandoah Mine sat at 12,198 feet near the head of the Dives Basin, a glaciated cirque below 13,416-foot Little Giant Peak, about four miles east of Silverton. It mainly produced lead. The most likely route between Silverton and the mine would have wound 4.5 miles up the Animas River Valley, then south 3.3 miles along Cunningham Creek, and finally uphill another 0.75 mile into Dives Basin.

The March 16, 2012, *Durango Herald* featured a retrospective on the slide based in large part on a survivor's account that first appeared in the *Silverton Standard* on April 7, 1906. William "Bill" Hall's testimony doesn't clear up the confusion over where the men were when the slide hit, but it paints a vivid picture of the immediate aftermath. "The slide struck us with the swiftness of a thunderbolt," Hall said. "There was no forewarning, nothing. We were out in the snow, struggling like drowning men—swept along, sometimes on top, sometimes underneath, helpless as a feather in a whirlwind."

When the slide stopped, two other miners, S. F. Nelson and Ed Fiance, saw Hall's head sticking out of the snow and pulled him free. The men then rescued Kid Teague, Joe Bradshaw, and others. In all, twenty-one men were caught in the Shenandoah-Dives avalanche, and twelve perished.

According to the *Durango Herald*, the Shenandoah-Dives slide was only one of many avalanches that struck the region that same day. Another wall of snow hit the nearby Green Mountain Mill, killing six men. And north of Silverton, George Marcott and Robert McIntyre were huddled around a "red-hot" woodstove up Burns Gulch when a slide slammed into their cabin. Marcott was killed when he was crushed against the stove and horribly burned, and McIntyre also died, bringing the day's death toll to twenty.

TWIN LAKES DOUBLE TRAGEDY, 1962

On the drier side of the Continental Divide and in the shadow of Colorado's tallest peak, 14,440-foot Mount Elbert, the village of Twin Lakes averages only twenty inches of precipitation a year. But January 1962 wasn't average. The month began with a big storm that dumped more than three feet of snow in the mountains above town. Then temperatures plummeted to 28 degrees below zero, leaving the fresh snow loose and unsettled. On Thursday, January 18, another storm blew in, bringing heavy snow and strong winds, with gusts up to seventy miles per hour. Snow continued to pile up into the weekend.

Two families, the Adamiches and the Sheltons, hunkered down in their homes just west of town along Colorado Highway 82 at the base of 12,682-foot Parry Peak, which marks the end of a ridge that spurs off Mount Elbert. A neighbor, Nils Lindstone, was sitting out the storm in his mobile home, while his renter, Jack Rowe, huddled in a cabin next door, both just west of the Shelton home. Two other nearby cabins were vacant. Other neighbors were snuggled into their cabins farther up and down the road. On Saturday, General Lee (his given name) Shelton plowed his neighbors' driveways. Bill Adamich tended to a cow and calf in his barn, the last of his dairy herd. The Adamich home sat on the south side of the highway next to a large meadow on the shore of Upper Twin Lake. When Bill finished feeding the cows, he trudged back to the house to join his wife, Barbara; their two sons, Billy, aged eight, and Michael, seven; and their pregnant dog, Pepe.

When Shelton finished plowing, he returned to his cozy home and his wife, Marie, and their children, Steve, aged fifteen, Linda, ten, and Vicki, seven. The Shelton home sat on the north side of the road at the mouth of Gordon Gulch, a slightly twisting, glacier-carved gully dropping from the north flank of Parry Peak. Given the heavy snow and high winds, General must have pondered the avalanche risk that day. He had heard old stories of avalanches in Gordon Gulch, but a 100-foot-high moraine stood between the bottom of the gulch and his home. Surely it would block any slide. General may not have known that at least three prior slides in Gordon Gulch—in 1899, 1916, and 1929—had been deadly, killing a total of four miners.

The next morning, Sunday, January 21, neighbors Bud and Edith Davis were awakened by a loud noise. Their electricity went off, but a clock marked the time at 5:31 A.M. Thinking the storm must have toppled a power line, they decided to wait till daylight to investigate. Neighbor Lindstone slept through the night, finally stepping outside after breakfast when he heard Rowe open his cabin door at 8:30 A.M. The two men stood gaping at where the neighbors' homes had been just the day before. In their place, the men saw nothing but deep snow mixed with broken trees, piles of shattered lumber, random bits of furniture and kitchen appliances, and battered cars. A massive avalanche had obliterated the handful of homes.

Rowe walked to the Twin Lakes store to telephone for help, but the phone line was dead. Then a couple of skiers in a car came up the road. They turned around and drove eight miles back to the town of Granite to get help. Other neighbors from up the road started digging through the debris, searching for survivors. More people came to help, and soon they could hear muffled cries. About five hours after the slide, Bill and Barbara Adamich were pulled alive—bruised, cut, and frostbitten—from the scattered wreckage of their home. A "wave" of snow had shoved them upward and under the rafters of their collapsed roof. Bill remembered waking to a sound like thunder and then a flash of light. The next thing he knew, he was pinned beneath a door in a small pocket of air. A prayer book that had been on a bedroom dresser somehow ended up on his chest. He hollered for help and prayed. Ambulances took Bill and Barbara to the hospital in Leadville.

Searchers found the lifeless body of Billy Adamich thirty feet away under only a foot of snow and rubble. Michael remained missing as 500 people probed the huge search zone. The avalanche was 1,000 feet wide when it crossed the road, and it ran another 1,000 feet into the meadow toward Upper Twin Lake. The compacted snow and debris lay ten to twenty feet deep.

General Shelton's brother Joe owned a vacation cabin and garage directly uphill from General's home. Joe and his family lived in Glenwood Springs and had planned to spend the weekend at their cabin, but work and bad roads had kept them at home. Joe Shelton said, "If it hadn't been for that, we probably would have been buried here, too." The slide demolished Joe's cabin and then shoved General's home off its foundation before collapsing and burying it. Searchers with shovels and probes eventually found the Sheltons—first Steve, beneath ten feet of debris, then General and Marie, across the road and down in the meadow. They then uncovered Linda and Vicki. Improbably, all of the Sheltons' bodies were still in their beds, under sheets and blankets, despite their home exploding around them and being swept far downhill. Linda and Vicki were found "locked in each other's arms as if they had a few seconds to grab for each other when their home took the avalanche's direct hit."

As darkness fell, another storm rolled in, suspending the search. Michael Adamich's body wasn't found until Tuesday, January 23, buried under twelve feet of snow and debris.

The Adamiches' cow and calf survived and were moved to a nearby farm. Their dog, Pepe, a terrier-Pekinese-bulldog mix, not only survived but soon gave birth to seven healthy puppies, an event dubbed the "Miracle of Mount Elbert." The puppies were auctioned off by the local American Legion post and radio station KBRR. With additional proceeds from a benefit basketball game in Leadville and other donations, the community raised nearly $7,000 for the survivors.

Bill Adamich was released from the hospital seven days after the slide, and Barbara four days after Bill. They moved in with Bill's mother in Leadville, but eighty-one-year-old Frances Adamich died two weeks later. The couple remained in Leadville until 1981 and eventually moved to Olympia, Washington. Reflecting on their tragedy, Barbara said, "The avalanche was a devastating thing. . . . You don't ever get over losing your children. . . . We were amazed at the kindness, compassion, and neighborliness of people and the love that poured out and is still left in our hearts."

SOURCES

Crutchfield, James A. *It Happened in Colorado: Remarkable Events that Shaped History.* Globe Pequot Press, 2008.

Grace, Stephen. *It Happened in Denver.* Two Dot/Globe Pequot Press, 2007.

Spilsbury, Louise, and Richard Spilsbury. *Crushing Avalanches.* Chicago, IL: Heinemann Library, 2003.

Spilsbury, Richard. *The Science of Avalanches.* New York, NY: Gareth Stevens Publishing, 2013.

Varney, Philip. *Ghost Towns of Colorado.* Voyageur Press, 1999.

December Blizzard, 1913

Breitenstein, Morgan. "The Biggest Snowstorm in Denver History, 1913." Denver Public Library, Western History Collection, March 2, 2015.

Kesting, Amanda. "On this day in 1913 Denver saw its biggest blizzard ever." NBC News 9, December 5, 2017.

Konrade, Laura. "The Record Setting Snowstorm of 1913 was the Biggest Blizzard in Denver History." Only In Your State, February 21, 2018.

Tosches, Rich. "Remembering Denver's Great Blizzard of 1913, a century later." *Denver Post*, November 29, 2013.

St. Patrick's Day Blizzard, 2003

"2003 Blizzard." National Weather Service, no date.

CPCU Society. "Statistics and Observations on the Colorado Blizzard of 2003." *Claims Quarterly*, December 2003.

Sneeringer, Breanna. "Looking Back: 82 inches of snow and $93 million in damages during 2003 blizzard." *OutThere Colorado*, March 11, 2021.

Sylte, Allison. "Remembering the March 2003 blizzard." NBC News 9, March 17, 2016.

The First Hall Valley Avalanche, 1877

Atkins, Dale. "A History of Colorado Avalanche Accidents, 1859–2006." *Proceedings of the 2006 International Snow Science Workshop, Telluride, Colorado.*

Woodstock Avalanche, 1884

McKee, Spencer. "Looking back at the 1884 avalanche that killed more than a dozen in Colorado." *OutThere Colorado*, November 13, 2018.

Homestake Mine Slide, 1885

"The Buried Colorado Miners." *The New York Times*, April 27, 1885.

"Homestake Mountain, CO Snow Slide Feb 1885." *Dallas Daily Herald*, April 28, 1885. Submitted to GenDisasters.com by Stu Beitler.

Silver Plume and the Big Snow Winter, 1898–1899

Echols, Mike. "When the 10 Italians died in a mighty avalanche." *Clear Creek Courant*, February 15, 1984.

Gilliland, Mary Ellen. "Summit's Historic Yesterdays: Winter of 1898–'99 buries town under 20 feet of snow." *Summit Daily*, December 21, 2015.

"Two Mighty Avalanches Sweep Down." *San Francisco Call*, February 13, 1899.

Liberty Bell Mine Avalanches, 1902

"Snow Slide Carries Away Buildings at the Liberty Bell Mine." *Daily Journal*, February 28, 1902.

Shenandoah-Dives Slide, 1906

"St. Patrick's disaster of 1906." *Durango Herald*, March 16, 2012.

Twin Lakes Double Tragedy, 1962

Chickering, Sharon. "Twin Lakes Tragedy." *Colorado Central Magazine*, January 1, 2000.

Martinek, Marcia. "Avalanche of 1962 is still in people's minds." *Herald Democrat*, January 24, 2008, reprinted February 19, 2014.

CHAPTER 9

ROCKFALLS AND LANDSLIDES

ROCKFALLS AND LANDSLIDES AREN'T UNCOMMON IN COLORADO, which is not surprising given the state's many steep-sided canyons and vast sea of mountains. Fortunately, that same rugged terrain tends to limit how many people might be in harm's way at any given time. Many such gravity-fed events cause no harm, but injuries and fatalities do occasionally occur, principally among mountaineers, rock climbers, and hikers who venture into precipitous country. According to the U.S. Geological Survey, rockfalls and landslides kill an average of twenty-five to fifty people each year in the United States. Colorado sees its share of such fatalities, including nine in 2010 alone.

In fact, 2010 got off to an ominous—though nonlethal—start. Glenwood Canyon's steep walls often spawn rockfalls that force the closure of Interstate 70, which runs through it. Just before midnight on Sunday, March 7, 2010, a huge rockslide, with some boulders the size of tractor-trailers, rumbled down the side of Glenwood Canyon just west of Hanging Lake Tunnel, damaging a bridge and closing the interstate. No injuries were reported, but the road remained closed for weeks, and the detour involved traveling an extra 200 miles, a huge inconvenience for motorists. For truckers, it caused delays and extra costs. Geologists for the Colorado Department of Transportation (CDOT) hurried to the scene but then had to walk two hours each way to inspect the slide. They found the slide area to be unstable. Governor Bill Ritter declared a disaster and asked

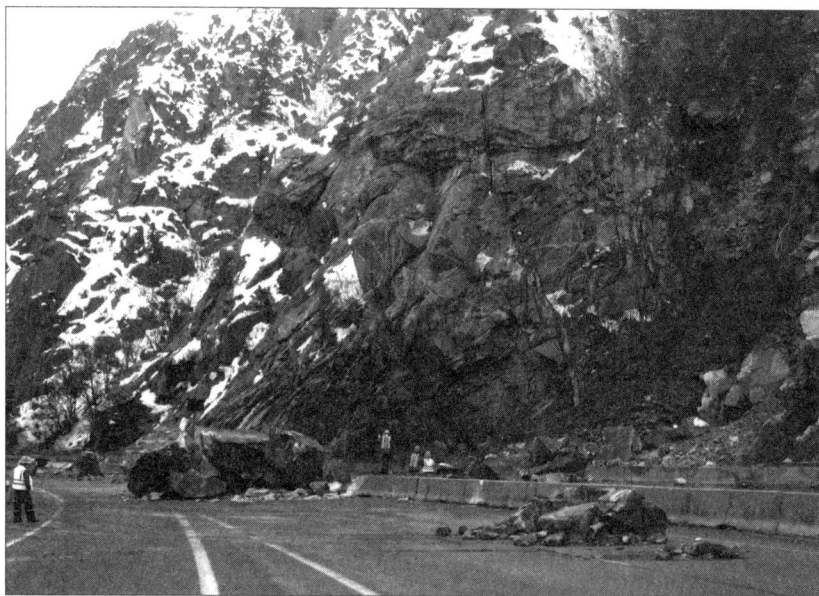

Crews work to clear rock debris from Interstate 70 in Glenwood Canyon. PHOTOGRAPH BY LYNN HIGHLAND, COURTESY OF THE COLORADO DEPARTMENT OF TRANSPORTATION.

the Federal Highway Administration to help pay for repairs. A similar rock-slide in the same area in 2004 had cost $700,000. Officials expected the repair bill this time to top $1 million. After the 2004 slide, they had been able to reopen the road the next day because they didn't have to deal with unstable ground above the slide.

The longest closure in this spot occurred in 2016. On February 15, rocks began to cascade down the flank of the canyon near the exit to Hanging Lake, which is about eight miles east of the town of Glenwood Springs. As many as twenty boulders ranging in size from three to ten feet in diameter fell onto the roadway. The largest of these weighed sixty-six tons and was the size of a Volkswagen. Typically, that section of roadway carries 25,000 vehicles a day.

The slide smashed into a passing tractor-trailer truck, but no one was injured. It damaged 120 feet of steel guardrail and 100 feet of median. CDOT crews removed 400 tons of rock and earth, rebuilt the road, repaired guardrails, and built new barriers to try to prevent future slides. Because of the repair work, I-70 remained closed for ten days, after which traffic was reduced to one lane with a pilot car, open only from 4 P.M. to 9 A.M., with up to four-hour delays. An option was to take a four-hour detour through Craig and Steamboat Springs. Traffic didn't return to normal for more than a month.

According to the Colorado Geological Survey, this section of road is one of the worst for rockfalls in the nation's entire interstate highway system. The Hanging Lake area is the deepest part of Glenwood Canyon. The base of the steep walls is made up of 1.7-billion-year-old rocks, including ancient granite. On top of these rocks is a layer of sandstone that is 500 million years old. After the granite formed but before the sandstone was laid down, there were millennia when no sediment accumulated, leaving the granite exposed to the forces of nature. Weathering weakened the granite and produced grooves and cracks in the rocks. It is here that most of the rockfalls occur, as water seeps into the cracks, expands with temperature changes, and further erodes them.

Certainly not all of Colorado's rockfalls and landslides occur in Glenwood Canyon, and not all involve tons of loosened rock. Sometimes, even a lone boulder can cause a tragedy. Just two days after the massive 2010 Glenwood Canyon slide, on March 10, Karen Lynn Evanoff was in exactly the wrong place at precisely the wrong time. Evanoff, a resident of Craig, was a passenger in a friend's 2004 Buick, commuting to her job as a housekeeper at The Phoenix Condominiums in Steamboat Springs. Just east of Hayden on U.S. Highway 40, their car passed a cliff face at 7:15 A.M., and a basketball-sized rock landed on the roof of the car. Fifty-six-year-old Evanoff was killed instantly; the driver of the car was uninjured. The boulder crushed the passenger-side roof, but somehow the driver was able to pull over safely.

CDOT engineers and a geologist inspected the cliff side after the accident and determined that there was no further immediate danger. Records showed that there had been no serious rockfalls in the area since 1998, so the road remained open, carrying not only its usual traffic but also motorists detouring around the massive rockslide on I-70 that had occurred two days earlier.

One news report mentioned that highway work crews had seen a herd of elk atop the cliff the day of the rockfall, but the elk may not have been to blame for the slide. Bob Barrett, a landslide specialist and chief geologist for I-70 through Colorado and Wyoming, said that natural weathering and the freeze-thaw cycle common in springtime was more likely what loosened the boulder from its resting place.

Even small rockfalls are a danger to climbers and hikers in Colorado's mountains. Near noon on September 26, 2010, thirty-year-old John Arthur Merrill of Cortez was killed by falling rock while climbing with his dog, Oof, at about 13,500 feet on El Diente Peak in southwest Colorado. Several rocks falling from above caused massive head injuries. Another hiking party saw the accident and ran to him, but by the time they reached him, Merrill was dead. The next day, a helicopter crew retrieved the body, which had to be "longlined," that is, carried by a cable hanging from the helicopter. The helicopter then returned to the peak to pick up rescue volunteers but was forced to make an emergency landing. Fortunately, no one was injured.

Merrill's dog, an Alaskan Malamute mix, was not injured in the rockfall and refused to leave its master; it spent the night on the mountain guarding the body. Merrill's wife, who was pregnant at the time, said her husband had phoned her shortly before the accident to tell her that he was about an hour from the top of the mountain. After the tragedy, she returned to her family in Guatemala and was unable to take the dog with her. One of the rescuers offered to adopt Oof.

El Diente Peak would have been Merrill's fifteenth "14er" (a peak over 14,000 feet in elevation), had he reached the top. His death was the second rockfall fatality on El Diente that year. Just two months earlier, fifty-nine-year-old Peter Topp, a retired U.S. Army colonel and experienced mountaineer from Colorado Springs, was killed while traversing the ridge between El Diente and Mount Wilson. Two companions were injured and rescued by helicopters in a "desperate" effort hampered by frequent "pounding" thunderstorms.

One of Colorado's deadliest rockslides occurred in September 2013, as a family from Buena Vista was hiking near Agnes Vaille Falls in Cascade Canyon, at the base of Mount Princeton, west of Nathrop. A half-mile trail there leads to a viewpoint below the falls, which were named for Agnes Wolcott Vaille, a prominent Denverite and early member of the Colorado

Mountain Club. (Before her death at thirty-four, Vaille summitted all fifty-four of the state's 14ers. She died in 1925 during a winter ascent of the east side of Longs Peak. A climbers' shelter near Longs' summit also bears her name.) The waterfall trail is popular, especially when snowmelt feeds the falls in springtime. But rockfall is an ever-present danger, as evidenced by the rubble-covered ground.

On September 30, 2013, Dwayne and Dawna Johnson, forty-six and forty-five respectively, were sightseeing with their daughters, Kiowa-Rain, eighteen, and Gracie-Faith, thirteen, and their cousins who were visiting from Missouri, Baigen Walker, ten, and Paris Walkup, twenty-two. As they neared a viewpoint below Vaille Falls, rocks came tumbling down the mountainside without warning. Some were the size of cars. Another hiker who saw the rockslide immediately called 9-1-1. He said it looked as if "a whole chunk of the mountain came down." When Chaffee County Sheriff's Deputy Nick Tolsma arrived on the scene, he heard a scream and saw a small hand sticking out of a pile of rubble. He dug Gracie out, and she was airlifted to a Denver hospital with a broken leg and other injuries. Other searchers dug by hand and eventually recovered the lifeless bodies of Gracie's father, mother, sister, and cousins. Gracie told her rescuers that her father had thrown himself on top of her as the rocks began to rain down on them. In all, an estimated 100 tons of boulders crashed down, covering an area the size of half a football field.

The town of Buena Vista, just thirteen miles from Agnes Vaille Falls, mourned the loss of the beloved family. Dwayne Johnson had worked as an electrician and had been an assistant football coach at Buena Vista High School, where his wife Dawna had coached track between two waitressing jobs. The school held a candlelight vigil in honor of the family. "We may never get over this," said family friend Jennifer Eggleston. "They were so much a part of every single thing we ever did. You won't be able to find a single person in this town that they did not touch."

Gracie's cousins also left behind grieving family and friends. According to an obituary, "Baigen's teachers could not say who his best friends were because he was kind to anyone around him and everyone felt like his best friend." Paris had played football at Avila University in Kansas City, Missouri, and had completed a nursing degree there that spring. He was remembered as "humble about his accomplishments and a good friend to many."

The direct cause of the rockfall remains unknown, but recent heavy rains may have been a contributing factor. The U.S. Forest Service has since rerouted the trail and posted signs warning visitors not to proceed beyond the viewpoint. Gracie recovered from her injuries and competed as a sprinter and hurdler on her high school track team, as well as played basketball. Her uncle Daryle, aunt Dayna, and cousin Tyler moved to Buena Vista so Gracie could live with them while she finished school. She also had the support of her brother, Dakota, who was not on the hike that fateful day.

Mudslides often cover a large area since they flow more readily than rockslides. As a result, they can be more destructive and, when they strike populated areas, deadlier, as demonstrated by a March 2014 mudslide near Oso, Washington, that killed forty-three people and made national headlines. Just two months later, on Sunday evening, May 24, 2014, a much larger mudslide struck near Collbran, about forty miles east of Grand Junction. Dubbed the West Salt Creek landslide, it began on a flank of Grand Mesa and ran for three miles, creating a channel a half mile wide and up to 250 feet deep. Fortunately, the locale was rural and sparsely

The West Salt Creek mudslide carved a massive chunk out of Grand Mesa. PHOTOGRAPH BY JON WHITE, COURTESY OF THE COLORADO GEOLOGICAL SURVEY.

inhabited. Nevertheless, three people died when they were caught in the massive debris flow.

Early that weekend, a local rancher had noticed that something had interrupted the flow of irrigation water to his fields near West Salt Creek. Three men from the community of Collbran volunteered to investigate: Wes Hawkins, forty-six, who worked for the local water district; Clancy Nichols, fifty-one, a Mesa County road and bridge employee; and Clancy's son, Danny Nichols, twenty-four. They found that a small mudslide had blocked an irrigation ditch. While they were inspecting the damage, a second, much larger mudslide broke loose from higher on the mesa. Nearby residents said it roared like a freight train. The U.S. Geological Survey reported that the slide covered eight square miles and triggered a 2.8-magnitude earthquake.

Searchers hoping to find the three men were hampered by unstable ground—the upper part of the slide moved another twenty feet overnight. The following morning, ground searchers could scout only the edges, so spotters used airplanes and drones with infrared cameras to conduct an aerial search. There was no trace of the missing men or their vehicle.

The slide's sheer headscarp reveals the surface that soils released from after being saturated by heavy rains. PHOTOGRAPH BY JON WHITE, COURTESY OF THE COLORADO GEOLOGICAL SURVEY.

Investigators noted that more than an inch of rain had fallen in that area over the weekend, with possibly higher amounts on top of Grand Mesa. The land that broke away was part of a bowl-shaped ridge that likely funneled precipitation into the steep, unstable soils. The upper fracture zone of the slide left a high, sheer wall. A year later, geologists said the ground was still unstable and would likely slide again. Hawkins and the two Nichols men were never found.

SOURCES

Banda, P. Solomon. "Search Continues for 3 Missing after Massive Mesa County Mudslide." Associated Press, CBS 4 Denver, May 27, 2014.

Beaudin, Matthew. "Search and Rescue removes hikers; one killed by rockfall." *Telluride Daily Planet*, July 27, 2010.

Boyer, Brent. "Woman killed when boulder hits car near Mount Harris on Wednesday." *Craig Press*, March 10, 2010.

Cook, Terri. "Why Glenwood Canyon is Prone to Rockfalls." *5280*, February 25, 2016.

Highland, Lynn M. "Landslides in Colorado, USA: Impacts and Loss Estimation for the Year 2010." U.S. Geological Survey, U.S. Department of the Interior.

"I-70 Glenwood Canyon Rockslide." Colorado Department of Transportation, online updates, March 8 through April 14, 2010.

Langlois, Krista. "Massive Colorado mudslide nearly clobbered gas wells." *High Country News*, May 28, 2014.

McGhee, Thom. "Rockslide closes 17 miles of I-70 in Glenwood Canyon." *Denver Post*, March 8, 2010.

Nicholson, Kieran, and Yesenia Robles. "2nd climber this year killed by rock slide on El Diente Peak in SW Colorado." *Vail Daily*, September 29, 2010.

Paris Delane Walkup obituary. Yarber Mortuary, Mountain View, Missouri.

Shoichet, Catherine E., Kyung Lah, and Jack Hannah. "Colorado rockslide kills 5 members of one family; teen survives." CNN, October 2, 2013.

Zennie, Michael, and Louise Boyle. "Rock slide survivor, 13, reveals how heroic father sacrificed himself to shield her from falling boulders before being killed along with 4 other family members." *Daily Mail*, December 5, 2013.

CHAPTER 10

EARTHQUAKES

COLORADO MAY NOT SPRING TO MIND WHEN YOU THINK OF EARTHQUAKES
—large quakes aren't as common in the Centennial State as they are, say, in California. But noticeable earthquakes do occasionally strike. The Colorado Geological Survey estimates that, since 1867, the state has experienced about 700 earthquakes of magnitude 2.5 or greater on the Richter scale. Most of these temblors were associated with the Rio Grande Rift, which runs north to south through the mountainous center of the state. Thousands of faults are part of the rift system, and about ninety of those are considered active.

The first quake recorded in Colorado history occurred on December 7, 1870, when, as geologist F. A. Hadsell reported, "A careful observer at Fort Reynolds, 20 miles east of Pueblo, noted that bottles standing 1 inch apart were knocked together violently." The first large quake to make headlines struck on November 7, 1882, centered about ten miles north of Estes Park. Because it happened so long ago, before there were accurate measuring instruments and careful record keeping, the quake was not well documented. But researchers now estimate that it was a magnitude 6.5. Ground movement was so severe that it snapped off the bolts anchoring Denver's electric generators, knocking out power, and it also cracked the walls of buildings in Boulder. The 1882 earthquake was likely felt as far west as Salt Lake City and as far east as Salina, Kansas. A report published by the Colorado Geological Survey stated, "This earthquake was probably the largest to occur in Colorado during the period of historic record. A similar-sized event today could have significant impact on modern structures, possibly causing serious property damage and perhaps injury or death."

Fortunately, most quakes that occur in Colorado are relatively small, causing only minor damage. The U.S. Geological Survey Earthquake Hazards Program rates Colorado's risk as low to moderate.

The state's other claim to earthquake fame rests on the fact that the National Earthquake Information Center is housed in Golden, ten miles west of Denver. Here, researchers process seismographic data from around the world whenever a quake occurs and rapidly provide it to agencies, scientists, and the public. The center also maintains an earthquake database and conducts research to better understand quake mechanisms.

Although the 1882 earthquake was Colorado's strongest to date, several other significant quakes have occurred over the years. In late August of 2011, a swarm of quakes hit the towns of Segundo and Valdez, about twelve miles west of Trinidad. Several small tremors rattled the area on August 21 and continued into the next day.

Then, on August 22, a 5.3-magnitude quake with an epicenter nine miles southwest of Trinidad struck at four minutes before midnight. Dean Moltrer and his brother Ray owned the Big 4 Country Store in Valdez. "This was the first time you could see the fear in people's eyes," Dean said. "Your family looks to dad to figure out what to do," added Ray. "Dad didn't know what to do. Dad was scared for his life."

In nearby Segundo, the quake shook pictures off of walls and dishes out of cabinets, cracked plaster walls, and shattered a chimney and a building's brick façade, both of which landed in the street. The Las Animas County Sheriff's Department had reports of a collapsed roof and porch, as well as small rockslides onto local roads and highways. Ringo's Super Trading Post in Segundo was closed the next day because the quake had knocked liquor bottles and groceries off shelves. Daylight shone through fresh cracks in the building's walls.

In Trinidad, Melissa Mestas, a barista at Café What A Grind said, "The whole house shook, the bookshelves, the paintings. It was really scary and just this helpless feeling." The historical building housing the coffee shop was damaged, as were several other old stone and brick buildings in town.

The quake was felt as far away as Greeley and southwestern Nebraska. In Englewood, Colorado, a student-built seismograph at Kent Denver

The brick façade of this building in Segundo collapsed during the earthquake. PHOTOGRAPH BY MATT MORGAN, COURTESY OF THE COLORADO GEOLOGICAL SURVEY.

School captured the Trinidad earthquake, adding excitement to the first day of the new school year for a group of seventh graders in an earth-science class.

Gavin Hayes, a seismologist at the National Earthquake Information Center, explained that, though this earthquake was strong for Colorado, it was not unexpected. A fault runs beneath Segundo to the northeast for more than three miles. In fact, a swarm of a dozen smaller quakes had hit the same area in 2001, and then two magnitude-4.5 quakes occurred on the same fault in 2016.

Not all Colorado quakes are natural. Geologists have confirmed that some earthquakes are "induced," primarily when liquid byproducts of fracking or other industrial activity are pumped at high pressure back into the ground. The first documented instance of induced seismic activity occurred in Colorado during the 1960s, in the region around Rocky Mountain Arsenal, northeast of Denver.

The federal government manufactured conventional and chemical weapons (including mustard gas and the nerve gas sarin) at the arsenal starting in the 1940s and then in the 1960s began leasing facilities to private companies that made pesticides on the site. Initially, liquid waste was held in ponds, but safety and environmental concerns led the government to dig a two-mile-deep injection well for waste disposal. The well was drilled in 1961, and the arsenal began pressure-injection of wastewater into the rock in March the next year. Within months, the residents of what had been a seismically quiet region began feeling one jolt after another. Over the next five years, the Denver area experienced 710 earthquakes, all with epicenters within a five-mile radius of the arsenal well. Then, in 1967, two quakes hit with a magnitude of over 5.0. The largest of these, at 5.3, caused an estimated $1 million in damage in Commerce City and north Denver. Windowpanes at Rocky Mountain Arsenal were shattered, Boulder schools closed when walls cracked, and other "minor" structural damage was widespread across the region.

A Denver-based geologist named David Evans charted the timing of local seismic activity compared to monthly wastewater injections (in millions of gallons) at the arsenal well and revealed an uncanny correlation. The more wastewater that was injected, the more frequent the quakes were. The federal government downplayed the evidence, and the U.S. Geological Survey (USGS) began collecting its own data, hoping to disprove Evans' study. In fact, the USGS data proved that Evans was right. The arsenal quit using the well and permanently sealed it in 1985. Incidentally, the President's Council on Environmental Quality awarded $50,000 to Evans for his work in bringing the issue to light.

USGS scientists found other areas in Colorado where injections were triggering earthquakes, notably the Rangely oil field in northwest Colorado. Water injections had been used there to improve oil recovery, and the injection area was soon experiencing as many as fifty minor quakes a day. Over a two-year test period, USGS found that when injections stopped, the number of daily quakes dropped to only ten a day. When injections started up again, the number of daily quakes went back to around fifty.

Although Colorado quakes have rarely reached the level of a major disaster, we know that sizable earthquakes will continue to occur. There may be unknown but potentially active faults in the state, and quakes will likely occur along known faults. With continued growth and development, more people and infrastructure will inevitably end up in harm's way. So even if Colorado's next quake isn't any greater in magnitude than previous ones, the scope of damage may exceed anything Coloradoans have seen before.

SOURCES

Associated Press. "Minor damage from magnitude-5.3 Colorado Quake." *Denver Post*, August 23, 2011.

Calhoun, Patricia. "Denver earthquakes 40 years ago were caused by Uncle Sam, not Mother Nature." *Westword*, August 24, 2011.

Colorado Geological Survey, *Rock Talk*, Vol. 5, No. 2. Division of Minerals and Geology. Colorado Department of Natural Resources.

Evans, David M. "The Denver Area Earthquakes and the Rocky Mountain Arsenal Well." *Mountain Geologist*, Vol. 3, 1966.

Hadsell, F. A. "History of earthquake activity in Colorado." *Colorado School of Mines Quarterly*, Vol. 63, No. 1, January 1968.

Steffen, Jordan. "5.4 quake in Trinidad, Colo., area unnerves region's residents." *Denver Post*, August 23, 2011.

Young, Quentin. "Colorado's Surprising History with Man-Made Earthquakes." *5280*, October 2016.

CHAPTER 11

AIRPLANE CRASHES

COMMERCIAL PASSENGER AVIATION FIRST CAME TO COLORADO WITH the completion of Colorado Springs Airport in 1927 and Denver Municipal Airport (later renamed Stapleton) in 1929. As air travel grew in popularity, airlines saw the state's central location and generally clear skies and decided it would make a good hub. Today, Denver International Airport is the third busiest airport in the United States and eighth busiest in the world, serving more than 60 million passengers a year. More than 35,000 people work at DIA, making it Colorado's largest employer.

Turbulence and unruly passengers notwithstanding, commercial flight is one of the safest ways to travel. In 2018, in the United States alone, more than 10.3 million scheduled flights carried a total of more than 1 billion passengers, with only one fatality. (A woman on a Southwest Airlines flight from New York to Dallas was partially sucked out a window when an engine exploded, cracked the window, and depressurized the cabin.) According to the U.S. Bureau of Transportation Statistics, the number of deaths per passenger mile for travelers on commercial airlines is 750 times lower than for travelers in cars and other vehicles. Nevertheless, when a plane falls from the sky, the results are often catastrophic.

WICHITA STATE FOOTBALL TEAM AIRPLANE CRASH, 1970

For many sports fans, fall means football. Collegiate and professional teams crisscross the country, traveling thousands of miles during a season to battle opposing teams. Typically, the only losses occur on the field, not en route to a game. But a team outing in 1970 took a tragic turn in the skies over Colorado.

The Wichita State University football team, the Shockers, regularly flew to away games and had chartered a Douglas DC-6B for the 1970 season. The four-engine DC-6 was large enough to carry the entire team and coaching staff. But that particular plane had been damaged in a windstorm, so the aviation charter company provided the team instead with two smaller aircraft.

The season got off to an inauspicious start. Leaving for a late September game against West Texas State, one of the Shockers' planes was damaged when its landing gear collapsed during takeoff at Oklahoma City. A second plane made two trips to bring the team home. To play against Utah State on October 3, the team chartered two twin-engine, forty-passenger Martin 404s from the Jack Richards Aircraft Company. It hired two pilots from Golden Eagle Aviation.

Excitement was high as the players and their luggage were loaded aboard the two 404s in Wichita on the morning of October 2, 1970. The Shockers had yet to win their first game of the season and were hoping for a victory that weekend against Utah State. The players nicknamed one of the planes "Gold" and the other "Black" after their school colors. The Gold passengers included athletic director Bert Katzenmeyer, head coach Ben Wilson, the university's admissions director, a ticket manager, state legislator Carl Fahrbach, several wives, and twenty-two starting players of the varsity team. The Black plane carried additional coaches, supporters, and football team members. Both planes carried luggage and team gear, and both planes landed at Stapleton Airport in Denver to refuel.

The flight plan called for them to continue on to Laramie, Wyoming, and then into Utah. Ronald Skipper, the president of Golden Eagle Aviation, was the pilot of the Gold plane and first officer, even though he did not have a rating for flying a Martin 404. He took the left seat, with Danny Crocker as copilot in the right seat. While on the ground at Stapleton, Skipper bought aeronautical charts for Loveland Pass. He then told the pilot of the Black plane that he was changing his route. The skies over Colorado were clear and calm; Skipper thought it was a fine day for sightseeing and wanted to give his passengers a look at the Rocky Mountains and fall foliage. The pilot of the Black plane followed the original flight plan to Logan, Utah. Skipper did not file a new flight plan for the Gold plane.

Skipper guided the Gold plane west up the Clear Creek Valley, pointing out to his passengers various peaks and landmarks. With the Continental Divide ahead, Skipper and the copilot realized that they had entered a box canyon. Motorists along Loveland Pass at about 11,900 feet elevation later reported being surprised to see an airliner in the valley about 1,000 feet below them near Dry Gulch. Another witness, a pilot familiar with the Loveland Pass area, was driving on U.S. Highway 6 east of the pass when he stopped his car to watch the Martin 404. He later said, "My initial and firm feeling was that the plane was in serious trouble as it was below the level of the mountains on either side that form the valley, and I didn't see how it could possibly turn around. Also, it was in nose-high altitude and flying at a low rate of speed, obviously straining to gain altitude, but barely keeping up with the rise of terrain."

The pilot and copilot knew they were in a serious predicament. The plane was too low and unable to climb above the ridges surrounding them on three sides. And the canyon was too confined for the plane to make a U-turn and reverse course. Skipper made a forty-five-degree turn to the right in an attempt to gain altitude. Copilot Crocker then yelled, "I've got the airplane," and made a sharp bank left. The aircraft stalled and lost altitude. According to survivors, the plane began to vibrate. Crocker lowered the nose of the plane. It clipped trees and slammed into the base of Mount Trelease. The impact ripped open the side of the plane, and there were two explosions, followed by smoke and fire. One passenger was ejected through the hole in the plane. A few others climbed through the hole, helping one another and collapsing in a heap about twenty feet from the wreck. Skipper, though suffering from head injuries, helped those who had escaped the wreckage to get farther away from the burning plane. Survivors reported that some people were conscious after the crash but were stuck under seats and debris and couldn't free themselves. The smoke, fire, and debris made it impossible for other survivors to reach those trapped inside.

Members of the Evergreen Mountain Rescue team carry a victim down the mountainside. PHOTOGRAPH COURTESY OF THE BUREAU OF AIRCRAFT ACCIDENTS ARCHIVES.

Mike Bruce, one of the least injured of the players, managed to climb out of the wreck and start down the mountain to get help. Construction workers building the Eisenhower Tunnel had seen the crash and started up the mountain. They met Bruce, who told them what had happened. Bruce continued downhill while the construction workers rushed toward the crash site. Bruce met a woman who took him to a construction-site office, where they called for help and she bandaged his leg. The construction workers heading up the hill met the other survivors heading down, some walking and some being carried, all injured and in burned clothing. The workers finally reached the site of the crash, where the plane had sheared off trees in a path that was 40 yards wide and about 100 yards long. Football helmets and pads lay strewn across the mountainside. Flames prevented these first responders from getting inside the airplane to search for any other survivors.

Those few survivors who had made it down to the highway were loaded into ambulances and taken to Idaho Springs, where they were given first aid by the sole doctor in town before being transferred to a Denver hospital. The team trainer, who had made it down the mountain, died of his burns in Idaho Springs. Army helicopters landed on the highway, ready to transport other survivors. The Georgetown and Idaho Springs fire departments arrived to fight the fire. Since water was not available, they used fire extinguishers and dirt to smother the flames. The fire had almost died when oxygen cylinders inside the aircraft exploded and started new fires. The body of the copilot, Crocker, was found near the base of a tree, where he had landed after being hurled from the plane.

When the Black plane landed without mishap and on schedule in Logan, Utah, passengers could see a number of cars at the airport. The offensive coach was called off the plane and told about the crash of the Gold plane. At that time, there was not an accurate count of survivors. Immediately, the coach returned to the plane and conducted a roll call. All of the passengers of the Black plane were taken to a hotel, where calls were made home to reassure friends and family of their safety. That night, they received a list of survivors from the Gold plane.

News of the crash reached Wichita via an Associated Press report that came over the wire to the KMUW radio station. Early reports of survivors were confusing. Since two planes were carrying the football team and supporters, it was not clear initially which of them had crashed and who was in each plane—or even who was piloting the Gold plane. Amid panic and shock, people scrambled to get accurate information. Classes at Wichita State University were canceled on Monday, and that night a memorial service was held in Cessna Stadium.

In all, thirty-three people died in the crash or soon afterward: fourteen players; fourteen staff, administrators, and boosters; the copilot; and two flight attendants. Two people who

A Wichita State University football helmet rests amid other wreckage at the crash scene. PHOTOGRAPH COURTESY OF THE BUREAU OF AIRCRAFT ACCIDENTS ARCHIVES.

survived the crash died a short time later from their burns and injuries. The pilot, Ronald Skipper, and eight players survived.

The game with Utah State was canceled, as was a game the following weekend with Southern Illinois. Without coaches, surviving football team members met on campus and voted on whether to continue the football season. All but one player voted to continue and dedicate the season to the memory of the plane-crash victims. Permission was given for freshmen team members to play on the varsity team. The Shockers played all their remaining games that season, but they lost every one.

This accident was one of the worst in Colorado aviation history. Four teams of investigators with the National Transportation Safety Board (NTSB) arrived at the scene the day after the crash. By late that Saturday afternoon, nineteen bodies had been recovered and placed in a makeshift morgue in Idaho Springs for identification. The search for victims continued until midnight and then resumed on Sunday morning. Meanwhile, the Federal Aviation Administration (FAA) impounded the second (Black) plane in Utah and inspected it. They found sixteen mechanical failures, including oil leaks in both engines and hydraulic-fluid leaks. The FAA immediately imposed a $50,000 fine on the Jack Richards Aircraft Company and rescinded the inspection certificate of the mechanic who had stated that the plane was airworthy.

Public hearings were held at the end of the month to determine the cause of the accident. Skipper testified for hours, but his response to most questions was "I don't recall." He said he had no idea why Crocker had grabbed control of the airplane just before the accident.

Eventually, the NTSB determined that the plane was carrying more weight than it could handle and that the engines did not have sufficient power for the quick altitude gain the situation demanded. The NTSB concluded that the accident could have been prevented, but a series of bad decisions led to the tragedy. Investigators found no evidence of mechanical failure of any kind. But in their report, officials noted the "overloaded condition of the aircraft, the virtual absence of flight planning for the chosen route of flight from Denver to Logan, and a lack of understanding on the performance capabilities and limitations of the aircraft." The report was critical of the pilot and copilot, who did not spend enough time examining the charts of their route before taking off in Denver. Had they done so, they would have known that the altitude they planned to fly at was too low to clear the Continental Divide. If the crew had acted minutes sooner, they could have made a successful turnaround.

Just five days after the accident, the first lawsuit was filed. Twenty-three other suits followed, most against Golden Eagle Aviation and the Jack Richards Aircraft Company. The FAA also bore significant responsibility for not following up on warnings it had recently issued to schools, including WSU, against using Golden Eagle's services. Years later, in 1977, WSU was found liable for not carrying sufficient insurance on its passengers, leading to more lawsuits against the university and its intercollegiate athletics association. In the end, victims' families received compensation from the NCAA and the State of Kansas.

Today, Memorial '70 on WSU's campus stands in memory of those who died in the crash. Every year on October 2, a wreath is placed at the monument. In Colorado, a roadside memorial with the victims' names was placed near the westbound lanes of Interstate 70 at Dry Gulch, about two miles east of the Eisenhower Tunnel. A trail leads up Dry Gulch to the crash site, where aircraft debris and downed trees remain on the slope. Over the years, friends and relatives of the victims have held special services there.

FLIGHT 1713 CRASH AT STAPLETON AIRPORT, 1987

In the 1920s, Mayor Benjamin Stapleton and Parks Department head Charles Vail championed a plan to build Denver Municipal Airport at the northeast edge of the city. It opened on October 17, 1929, just eleven days before Black Friday on Wall Street and the start of the Great Depression. Nevertheless, the facility proved financially viable, thanks in part to airmail flights, and by 1937 it served both United and Continental Airlines. In 1944, the airport was renamed Stapleton International.

By the 1980s, Denver and the city of Aurora to the south and east had grown around the airport, with homes and businesses encroaching on the boundary fences, particularly in the Park Hill and East Colfax neighborhoods. Stapleton was becoming obsolete. Hemmed in on all sides, it had no room to expand, and its runways were cramped, which caused long waits in bad weather when visibility was poor. Officials began planning to annex land and build a new, much larger airport in Adams County, farther northeast of the city.

Meanwhile, flights continued to arrive at and depart from Stapleton. On November 15, 1987, a winter storm warning was in effect, and the first significant storm of the season brought wet, heavy snow to the Denver metro area. By noon, Stapleton had six inches of snow on the ground, with more falling on strong crosswinds. As usual in such conditions, flights in and out of Stapleton were delayed. Continental Airlines Flight 1713, a DC-9, had arrived from Wichita, Kansas, and was scheduled to depart for Boise, Idaho, at 12:25 P.M. But its takeoff, like many others that day, was delayed by the weather.

On board were seventy-seven passengers and five crew members, including forty-three-year-old Captain Frank Zvonek Jr. He had 12,125 hours of flight experience but only 166 hours on a DC-9. He had been upgraded to captain only three weeks earlier. Zvonek's first officer was twenty-six-year-old Lee Bruecher, who had 3,186 flight hours, with only 36 on a DC-9. Bruecher had come to Continental just four months earlier after flying with Rio Airways, a small regional company based in Texas. Three flight attendants rounded out the crew.

At 1:03 P.M., in poor visibility and without notifying air-traffic controllers in the tower, Flight 1713 left the gate and taxied to the deicing pad, where deicing was completed by 1:46 P.M. Six minutes later, the pilot requested permission to "taxi from the ice pad." Believing that Flight 1713 was still at the gate, the tower cleared the pilot to taxi to the deicing pad. Having already completed deicing, the crew apparently took this as clearance to taxi to the runway. By 2:05 P.M., unbeknownst to the tower, Flight 1713 was in the "number one" spot, awaiting clearance for takeoff. While air-traffic controllers cleared other planes for takeoff, snow piled up on the wings of Flight 1713. Finally, the crew radioed the tower again and was cleared for takeoff at 2:14 P.M.

Airport officials and passengers on Flight 1713 later reported that the twin-engine DC-9 appeared to accelerate normally down the runway. Just as it became airborne, with Bruecher at the controls, the plane suddenly over-rotated and dropped, striking the ground with the left wing. The wing split from the fuselage, spraying fuel, and a fireball briefly flashed through the passenger cabin. The fuselage then slammed into the ground and skidded in the slush for 1,500 feet before overturning. The inverted tail acted as a lever to crush the main cabin. An airport official who observed the crash, Richard Boulware, said, "The whole fuselage twisted like a chicken whose neck was wrung." The jet lay upside down in a snowy field with clothing and luggage scattered across the ground. Several small fires broke out, and surviving passengers struggled to free themselves from the broken aircraft. Fortunately, the plane ended up near the airport firehouse, so responders were quickly on the scene and soon had the flames out.

The wreckage of Continental Flight 1713 lies on the ground at Stapleton International Airport.
PHOTOGRAPH COURTESY OF THE NATIONAL TRANSPORTATION SAFETY BOARD.

Twenty-three passengers died in the crash, most from blunt-force trauma or crushing. They ranged in age from six months to fifty-four years. Captain Zvonek, First Officer Bruecher, and one flight attendant, Diana Mechling, thirty-three, of Aurora, were also killed on impact. Two more passengers died in the hospital. Two of the flight attendants and fifty-two passengers survived; twenty-seven of them suffered major injuries.

At least a dozen city fire trucks responded to the crash, and staff from nearby Fitzsimons Army Medical Center in Aurora provided triage care. Near-blizzard conditions and the mangled condition of the airplane hampered rescue efforts, and some of the victims were trapped in the wreckage for more than five hours. First responders reported seeing dazed survivors wandering in the field among pieces of twisted metal. They were helped onto buses and taken to hospitals for treatment.

At 8:30 P.M., crews used two cranes to lift the rear of the plane and retrieve the last five bodies from the wreckage. Meanwhile, in Boise, family members and friends who had come to the airport there to meet passengers of Flight 1713 were taken into a banquet room to await news and hear the names of victims and survivors.

The accident report by the National Transportation Safety Board (NTSB) documented several odd twists of fate. No one sitting in a left-side window seat in rows 2 through 9 survived. Several passengers from this section, buckled into their assigned seats, were thrown from the airplane and killed, but the passenger in 8E, who had unbuckled his seatbelt and was sleeping when the plane took off, somehow remained in the fuselage and survived. Several passengers in the forward cabin escaped by crawling through breaks in the fuselage, while others were pinned in. A six-month-old infant on his mother's lap in seat 5C was killed, but his mother, seriously injured, survived.

Passengers in rows 10 to 15 suffered terrible crushing injuries, and some died of suffocation as a result. From row 15 to the rear of the plane, the fuselage was less compressed. The passenger seated in 22E was severely injured, but all of the passengers in the last three rows suffered only minor injuries. The only passenger wholly uninjured was a six-week-old infant held on her father's lap in seat 24E. When the tail-cone exit hatch was opened, some passengers were able to exit on their own; others required extrication.

A fifty-six-year-old orthopedic surgeon who survived the crash later said, "I thought I was going to die. It happened so slowly that I had time to think it three times. I just hoped it wouldn't hurt too much." He was trapped in the wreckage for two hours but escaped with only a broken finger. "I tried to think about other things—other trips, things in the past, my wife and family," he said. "Thanksgiving seemed to be an awfully good thing to think about."

Other survivors weren't as fortunate. Kenneth Watson, forty-five, an administrator and teacher at Northwest Nazarene College in Nampa, Idaho, suffered head injuries in the crash and was listed in critical but stable condition at an area hospital. He would recover and return home, but his rehabilitation was long and difficult.

An Idaho State University student aboard the flight was returning from a convention in Kansas City. She was seated in the middle of a row of three seats. When the plane crashed, she and the passengers on either side of her slid along the ground, strapped into their seats. When the seat section finally stopped, the student was able to unbuckle herself and stand. She suffered only cuts and bruises.

The two flight attendants who survived the crash were credited with remarkable courage as they ignored their own injuries and tried to help passengers. Flight attendant Kathy Engelhardt came upon one passenger who was pinned upside down. He was cold, so she rubbed his hands to warm him and then placed her own coat on him to ward off the chill. Once all the passengers were off the plane, Engelhardt was treated for her injuries and later released from the hospital.

The passengers also helped one another. One man said that both he and the passenger next to him were pinned and couldn't get out, but he was able to free his neighbor with the one arm he could move. As some passengers were crawling out, they paused to unbuckle others who could not help themselves. One of the first to exit the plane was a young man who then went back inside to help others who were trapped.

Both Continental Airlines and the NTSB investigated the crash, relying on information from the cockpit voice recorder and a flight data recorder. Continental Airlines' report cited wake turbulence, poor snowplowing of the runway, and errors on the part of traffic controllers. In contrast, the NTSB report noted that snow on the runway had not affected other flights; it also dismissed concerns over a wingtip vortex from a Boeing 767 landing on nearby runway 35R. The NTSB report concluded that Flight 1713 was adequately deiced but noted that twenty-seven minutes elapsed between deicing and takeoff. This was sufficient to raise the stall speed of the airplane and compromise its stability and the ability of the pilot to maintain control.

The NTSB pointed to other factors that contributed to the accident, including First Officer Bruecher's poor banking of the plane. Also noted was Bruecher's twenty-four-day layoff after his previous flight, which was deemed excessive given his lack of experience in a DC-9. The investigators also discovered that, prior to being hired by Continental, Bruecher had been fired from an air-taxi service for failing to pass a flight exam three times, despite twice the normal amount of training. His flight examiner told the NTSB that Bruecher had "chronic troubles," was easily disoriented, and was "unable to cope with deviations from the routine." After joining Continental, Bruecher's difficulties persisted. During a July 1987 simulator training session, he "completely lost control of [the] aircraft with [an] engine out at 2,000 feet."

The NTSB also found several decision-making deficiencies on the part of Captain Zvonek and questioned his pairing with Bruecher, since both had relatively little DC-9 experience. Finally, the NTSB cited procedural errors in communications between the flight crew and ground controllers.

As a result of this crash, Continental Airlines paid $20 million to settle thirty-six cases out of court. Kenneth Watson accepted payment from the settlement as part of his decision to move on from the crash. Because of his head injury, he doesn't remember that November day—or even much of the month. "I don't have the grimness of the crash in my mind," he said. But the incident still reverberates through his life. "I was on a professional track, and I was knocked off that track," Watson recalled later. "My mind got banged around, and it left me different." After more than a year in recovery, Watson did return to work at the college in a different capacity.

In a lawsuit that went to trial, the jury awarded $800,000 to a woman for her injuries sustained in the crash. But it did not cite the airline for negligence. Nonetheless, Continental updated its deicing procedures and instituted a system to prevent pairing inexperienced crew members on the same flight.

Stapleton Airport was decommissioned fewer than seven years later, and the area has since been redeveloped into a residential neighborhood with retail and open space. Suburban homes now dot the crash site between soccer fields and baseball diamonds.

SOURCES

Wichita State Football Team Airplane Crash, 1970

Allen, Robert. "Wichita State plane crash killing 31 in 1970 revisited Saturday." *Summit Daily*, August 14, 2010.

Garrison, Robert. "'Escape was not possible': 49 years ago, a football team's plane crashed in the Colorado mountains." ABC 7 Denver, October 3, 2019.

National Transportation Safety Board. *Aircraft Accident Report, Martin 404, N464M, 8 Statute Miles West of Silver Plume, Colorado, October 2, 1970.* File no. 3-1127.

"Wichita State University Plane Crash." Colorado Encyclopedia. Adapted from: Harner, Ariana. "'Scenic Route Through the Rockies': The Wichita State University Tragedy." *Colorado Heritage Magazine*, Vol 18, No. 1, 1988.

Flight 1713 Crash at Stapleton Airport, 1987

Associated Press. "Jetliner crashes on takeoff." Atchison *Daily Globe*, November 16, 1987.

Associated Press. "Pilot in Denver air crash had failed 3 flight exams." *Los Angeles Times*, September 27, 1988.

"Denver plane crash kills 26." *Chicago Tribune*, November 16, 1987.

National Transportation Safety Board. *Aircraft Accident Report, Continental Airlines, Inc., Flight 1713, McDonnell Douglas, DC-9-14, N626TX, Stapleton International Airport, Denver, Colorado, November 15, 1987.* PB88-910411.

Parker, Laura. "Denver jet was in air for seconds." *Washington Post*, November 17, 1987.

"Scars remain from DC-9 crash 2 years later." *Deseret News*, November 23, 1989.

Wheelan, John. "Jury Awards Woman $800,000 in Suit over Continental's 1987 Denver Crash." Associated Press, January 31, 1989.

CHAPTER 12

MASSIVE CAR PILEUPS

COLORADO IS A LARGE STATE, BUT WITH NEARLY 6 MILLION RESIDENTS and nearly 90 million visitors every year, traffic can get heavy, especially on major roadways in and around the bigger cities and towns. Combine that with steep mountain grades and volatile weather, and vehicle accidents are inevitable. Unfortunately, one hiccup in traffic can start a chain reaction that can involve dozens of cars and trucks, a phenomenon known as a pileup. Poor visibility, slick roads, high speeds, and motorists stressed by crowded highways are often contributing factors. Here are two of the more infamous pileups in Colorado history.

104-VEHICLE PILEUP ON I-25, 2014

On March 1, 2014, just before 11 A.M., a sudden, intense blast of snow surprised Denver motorists on a 1.5-mile stretch of Interstate 25 between Logan Street and University Boulevard. The dense curtain of snow accompanied an abrupt temperature drop, and vehicles quickly lost control on the now-slippery, flash-frozen pavement.

Cars and trucks were suddenly sliding in every direction. In this chaos, seventy-two-year-old Doug Newkirk desperately tried to maneuver his year-old Chevrolet Sonic, a subcompact. His sixty-one-year-old wife, Becky, was in the front passenger seat. They had driven to Colorado from Stillwater, Oklahoma, to reunite with twelve of Becky's fifteen siblings for their mother's ninety-third birthday. Doug later told reporters, "I've never been in a snowstorm that happened that quick or that bad, instantly. Seemed like you drove through a wall of snow. All at once, the car wouldn't steer, the car wouldn't stop, the car wouldn't do nothing is about what it amounted to." Helpless to change course, the Newkirks slammed into a jackknifed tractor-trailer and a concrete barrier. "We were going at that truck and there was nothing I could do about it," Doug said. Then a hard blow came from behind, crumpling the small red car. Bleeding and unconscious from the collision, Doug was helped at the scene by other victims and then loaded into an ambulance. He came to on the way to the hospital, wondering where he was and what had happened to Becky.

The pileup was called in as an MCI, or mass-casualty incident, and first responders, seeing smashed cars and metal strewn everywhere, expected many casualties. Remarkably, only thirty people, adults and children, were hospitalized. Two paramedics who happened to be nearby reached the accident scene quickly, pounded on the hood of each car, and talked to the occupants to determine who was most seriously injured.

In an interview the morning of the accident, Darrell Barber noted the sudden change in conditions as he drove his Chevy Tahoe on I-25. Barber was heading home that Saturday after shopping for his wife's retirement party. Roads were slick, he said. "Brake lights were coming on, and people weren't stopping." He explained that, a few cars ahead of him, he saw a tractor-trailer jackknife and slide into a concrete barrier along the edge of the far-right lane. The cars behind the semi tried to avoid it, but they collided and bounced off one another.

Barber was one of the few who managed to stop his vehicle, but a sliding sedan sideswiped the passenger side of his Tahoe. Then Barber saw a tow truck veer into the far-left passing lane to avoid stopped cars. The tow-truck driver lost control and slid into a jeep. Two cars following the truck slid into it, wedging beneath its bed. Then more cars jammed in from behind. As another car tried to avoid the tow-truck pileup, it swerved into the driver's side of Barber's Tahoe. Then an SUV slammed into the Tahoe's rear end and sent it flying forty feet onto the rear of a car carrier truck. Somehow Barber emerged unscathed.

Another motorist report-
ed that he ended up being part
of what he called "a Subaru
sandwich." Twenty-three-year-
old Carlos Davila was driving
home to Lakewood from work
in his Subaru Impreza. It was
his "affordable dream car,"
and he called it Mr. Rumbles
for the sound of the engine.
As Davila hit the patch of
bad weather and saw flashing

Unable to stop on the icy road, drivers ended up wedged together behind a tow truck on Interstate 25. PHOTOGRAPH COURTESY OF THE DENVER POLICE DEPARTMENT.

taillights ahead, he downshifted and hit the brakes. But he skidded out of control and slammed into a Subaru ahead of him. Then another Subaru struck Davila from behind, pushing his Impreza into the rear of the car ahead until Davila's windshield caved. Davila, groggy from the impact, managed to crawl out through the front passenger door. When first responders saw his car crushed between the other two, they expected to find another fatality. They were relieved to find the car empty and Davila nearby, relatively unhurt.

The pileup closed the northbound lanes for five hours. Traffic was diverted to nearby streets, which became crammed bumper to bumper. A heated passenger bus was brought in for the uninjured to sit in for interviews with investigators. Some people walked up an exit ramp to use the restroom in a nearby Whole Foods Market. One said that the normalcy of the grocery store was jarring in contrast to the mayhem of the accident scene.

The snow squall had been intense but brief. The National Weather Service reported that the metro area received only 0.75 to 1.5 inches—so little snow yet so much damage. Several motorists involved in the pileup said that some people were driving too fast even before conditions wors-ened. The police investigation was hampered by the ice and snow and a lack of skid marks on the pavement. It was also impossible to determine which cars had sped into others versus cars that had successfully stopped only to be hit from behind and pushed into other vehicles. In the end, the

Denver District Attorney's Office decided not to file any charges. The flash freeze had surprised everyone, and it was too difficult to pinpoint blame in what was one of the worst pileups in Denver history.

Despite the large number of vehicles involved and numerous injuries, remarkably only one person was killed. As he was being treated in the emergency room, Doug Newkirk overheard someone ask if anyone else had been in his car, and another voice replied something about a "DOA"—dead on arrival. What he had most feared was true: Becky, his wife of thirty-two years, had died at the scene. Newkirk didn't look for people to blame; he knew firsthand the helplessness of all the drivers in the pileup. And as a former truck driver, he empathized with the driver at the wheel of the jackknifed tractor-trailer. "That woman," he said, "she's got to have nightmares."

FIERY CRASH KILLS FOUR ON I-70, 2019

A smaller but deadlier pileup occurred on April 25, 2019, on Interstate 70, an east-west highway through Denver that connects the mountains with the plains. This incident began with a crash between a semi-truck and a school bus near Ward Road in Lakewood that resulted in minor injuries. But that accident blocked eastbound lanes on I-70, bringing traffic to a standstill at the start of the afternoon rush hour. By 4:50 P.M., the eastbound lanes were still bumper to bumper, with traffic moving at no more than ten miles per hour and backed up four miles to the Colorado Mills Parkway overpass. None of the gridlocked motorists realized the danger approaching from behind.

What they didn't know was that a flatbed semi-truck was careening out of control as it sped down I-70's steep grade east of the Genesee exit. The flatbed driver passed up a chance to use a gravel off-ramp designed to stop runaway trucks, instead veering across lanes of traffic, almost hitting a pickup truck. Then the flatbed entered a long straightaway, speeding east on I-70 toward Lakewood.

One driver with a dashboard camera caught what was about to happen next. Josh McCutcheon was stuck in traffic just west of the Colorado Mills Parkway overpass when his dashcam, facing rearward, recorded a flatbed semi-truck loaded with bundled lumber flashing by at high speed between the right lane and the guardrail. "Oh my god!" McCutcheon shouted. "We almost . . . died!"

People in the cars stopped below the overpass were not as fortunate. The racing flatbed had run out of open road. Pinched between the lanes full of vehicles and the guardrail, the flatbed, going an estimated eighty-five miles per hour, slammed into passenger cars and another semi-truck. (The flatbed driver later said that a semi-truck parked illegally on the shoulder forced him to swerve back onto the roadway.) Hit from behind, the gridlocked cars pinballed into one another. Lumber scattered across the roadway, gasoline tanks ruptured, and something sparked a fire. Lakewood police spokesman John Romero said, "It was crash, crash, crash and explosion, explosion, explosion." In all, the collision involved twenty-five cars and four semi-trucks. As cars and lumber burned, the plume of black smoke could be seen for miles.

Several people injured in the crash were fortunate that others came to their rescue. One who rushed in to help was Darin Barton, dubbed the "homeless hero," whose preferred panhandling spot was near the overpass. Barton saw the flatbed truck smash into several cars, and then the truck cab rolled over. "As soon as it rolled over, it just caught on fire," he said. "And I just dropped my sign, took off running"—not to safety but toward the fire. Barton pulled several people from their cars before the fire got to them. "I didn't do this all myself. There were other people in traffic that helped," he said. "I just did what I hope anybody would've done." Donations for Barton poured in to a local Fox News affiliate, and many people emailed the station to voice their gratitude for his selfless heroism.

The first car hit by the flatbed semi belonged to Leslie Maddox, a graphic designer at nearby Red Rocks Community College. She suffered a compound fracture of her arm, a badly broken nose, and lacerations to her forehead. "The whole front of my car was blown away," Maddox said. "There was glass everywhere." She was in so much pain, she didn't want to move. Then a young woman in a Red Rocks Community College T-shirt opened the door to Maddox's car. "You need to get out," she said. A man, identified only as Lloyd, joined them, saying, "You need to move, things are starting to blow!" Together, they moved Maddox to safety.

First responders did their best to save lives and battle the fire, but the heat and flames were so intense they could not check every car for victims before the fire engulfed the vehicles. The chief engineer for the Colorado Department of Transportation (CDOT), Josh Laipply, reported that the highway surface beneath the fire reached more than 2,500 degrees Fahrenheit, melting the pavement, tires, and even aluminum car parts. Four men were killed at the scene, and ten people with serious injuries were taken to a local hospital by West Metro Fire Rescue. A West Metro worker also received minor injuries when he was hit with debris from an exploding tire. Of the ten people hospitalized, all but one were released the next day.

Although the crash happened just before 5 P.M. on Thursday, an official tally of victims was not announced until Sunday, when the accident scene had cooled enough for investigators to make a thorough search. The Jefferson County Coroner's Office listed the four who had died in the accident: Doyle Harrison, sixty-one, of Hudson; William Bailey, sixty-seven, of Arvada; Stanley Politano, sixty-nine, also of Arvada; and Miguel Angel Lamas Arellano, twenty-four, of Denver.

Work crews made emergency repairs to the melted roadway, and engineers inspected the scorched overpass to make sure it was structurally sound. The investigation of the crash scene, combined with damage to the freeway surface and overpass, closed this stretch of I-70 for four days.

Within days of the crash, Leslie Maddox had surgery to repair her broken arm. Then she tracked down her two Good Samaritans to thank them. She had learned that Lloyd was a former Marine and the young woman, Melcia Harsch, was a student at Red Rocks in the school's emergency medical technician (EMT) program. Harsch, a mother of two and pregnant at the time, had been driving a new Jeep that was totaled in the crash. Ignoring her own injuries, she had helped rescue several people that day. Maddox has since stayed in touch with her and Lloyd.

Amazingly, the driver of the flatbed lumber truck suffered only minor injuries. Twenty-three-year-old Rogel Lazaro Aguilera-Mederos was a driver for Castellano 03 Trucking based in Houston, Texas. Born in Cuba, he had been a legal U.S. resident for several years. After the crash, Aguilera-Mederos was arrested on suspicion of vehicular homicide, but investigators soon concluded that the accident was not intentional, nor were alcohol or drugs involved. Aguilera-Mederos told authorities that his brakes failed as he sped down the mountain grade west of Lakewood. He tried emergency brakes, but they too failed. Aguilera-Mederos said he didn't drive off the road because he didn't want to roll his truck.

Police reviewed a dashcam video that apparently showed Aguilera-Mederos' semi-truck leaking what might have been brake fluid and then bypassing more than one runaway-truck ramp, as well as roadside signs warning drivers to check their brakes. Investigators also spoke with a couple who said that, hours before the crash, a semi-truck matching the description of Aguilera-Mederos' had passed them in a no-passing zone as they approached a curve in the road near Rand, a small town fifty miles south of the Wyoming border. They said it was trav-eling seventy to eighty miles per hour in a forty-five-mile-per-hour zone and almost ran them off the road.

Police arrested the driver of the run-away truck, Rogel Aguilera-Mederos, who said that his brakes had failed. PHOTOGRAPH COURTESY OF THE LAKEWOOD POLICE DEPARTMENT.

Aguilera-Mederos said he was headed back to Texas from Wyoming with a load of lumber. Castellano 03 Trucking was a small company with only five trucks and five drivers. It had been slapped with multiple maintenance viola-tions in the two years before this accident, including ten violations related to brakes. There had also been two "driver fitness" violations for not being able to read or speak English sufficiently to understand traffic signs and signals. During that period, however, the carrier's trucks were not involved in any fatal or injury-related crashes.

Aguilera-Mederos was charged with thirty-six felonies, a traffic misde-meanor, and three sentence enhancers. Among the charges were four counts of vehicular homicide, six counts of first-degree assault, and twenty-four counts of attempted first-degree assaults. Aguilera-Mederos' attorney, Rob Corry, argued that the truck had experienced a mechanical malfunction and the crash was an accident. Prosecutors countered that Aguilera-Mederos showed "extreme indifference" to human life.

In May 2019, Aguilera-Mederos pleaded not guilty to all charges. He was released on $400,000 bail, and he returned to Texas to live with his family. The case has stumbled along through several changes in attorneys representing Aguilera-Mederos, several postponed trial dates, attempts at a plea agreement, and delays caused by the COVID-19 pandemic. Finally, a trial date was set for early 2021. During the trial, Aguilera-Mederos testified that well before the crash he had stopped to check his brakes and found them to be working. When they eventually failed, his truck was only going forty-five miles per hour, but his speed increased on the downgrade coming into Lakewood. As he rolled toward the gridlocked traffic, he said, there was little he could do.

Nevertheless, in October 2021, a jury found Aguilera-Mederos guilty on forty-two counts, including four counts of vehicular homicide and six counts of assault in the first degree. In December, bound by state minimum-sentencing laws, District Court Judge Bruce Jones sentenced Aguilera-Mederos to 110 years in prison. The defendant's attorney immediately planned to appeal, and many people—even families of some of the victims—questioned the severity of the sentence, noting that the crash was unintentional. Even Judge Jones said he had no desire to see Aguilera-Mederos die in prison, adding, "If I had the discretion, it would not be my sentence." The *Denver Post*'s editorial board called for Governor Jared Polis to commute part of the sentence, and within days of the sentencing an online petition to grant clemency to Aguilera-Mederos had gathered more than 2 million signatures. By month's end, more than 5 million people had signed it. Finally, on December 30, 2021, calling the crash a "tragic but unintentional act," Governor Polis reduced Aguilera-Mederos' sentence from 110 years to 10.

Several victims of the crash settled for damages with the Castellano 03 Trucking Company, but it has since gone out of business. There seems to be little opportunity to further hold the now-defunct company accountable for either the truck's failed brakes or its driver's apparent lack of experience and insufficient training.

SOURCES

104-Vehicle Pileup on I-25, 2014

"Family and Friends Honor Stillwater Woman Killed in Denver Pileup." News 9 Oklahoma City, March 5, 2014.

Mitchell, Kirk. "I-25 pileup: 1 killed, 30 hospitalized after snowy disaster." *Denver Post*, March 1, 2014.

Simpson, Kevin. "I-25 Denver pileup: Vehicles, disparate lives collided in massive accident." *Denver Post*, March 22, 2014.

Fiery Crash Kills Four on I-70, 2019

Bachus, Kyle. "Vehicular Homicide—Understanding the I-70 Semi Accident." Car Accidents, Bachus Schanker, May 6, 2019.

"Good Samaritan Meleia Harsch Describes Rescue of Leslie Maddox, Other I-70 Driver." CBS 4 Denver, May 6, 2019.

Hindi, Saja. "Survivor of I-70 crash: 'My world had blown up in front of me.'" *Denver Post*, May 2, 2019.

Ismail, Adam. "Truck driver sentenced 110 years for deadly crash stemming from brake failure even though everyone agrees it's unreasonable." Jalopnik, December 16, 2021.

Kruegel, Evan. "Millions sign petition asking for reduced sentence for truck driver in I-70 crash." Fox News 8, December 17, 2021.

Madani, Doha. "Truck driver's sentence reduced from 110 years to 10 by Colorado governor in fatal crash." NBC News, December 30, 2021.

"Millions sign petition to change trucker's sentence." KMGH ABC News 25, Central Texas, December 18, 2021.

Nicholson, Kieran. "Company of truck driver arrested in fiery I-70 crash had multiple brake safety violations." *Denver Post*, April 29, 2019.

Rios, Joseph. "DA lays 40 charges on driver of deadly I-70 crash." Colorado Community Media, May 3, 2019.

Roberts, Michael. "Truck Driver in Massive Fatal I-70 Crash: 'This is Not Just, What They are Doing.'" *Westword*, May 1, 2019.

Turner, Shaul. "'Homeless hero' who rescued people from I-70 crash has saved lives before." Fox 31 News, Denver, April 30, 2019.

CHAPTER 13

WILDFIRES

AS IN OTHER STATES ACROSS THE WEST, WILDFIRES HAVE LONG BEEN a natural force in shaping Colorado's landscape. In recent years, however, the fire season has grown longer and fires have become larger, more destructive, and more costly. Scientists agree that a warming and more volatile climate is partly to blame. And ever-increasing development places more homes, businesses, and infrastructure—and people—in harm's way. Here are stories of recent wildfires that charred swaths of Colorado, including the state's largest wildfires to date and two blazes that incurred the greatest losses.

HAYMAN FIRE, 2002

In the Pike-San Isabel National Forests northwest of Colorado Springs, June 2002 started off abnormally hot and dry. For four days, temperatures rose into the 90s, and humidity was low. This came on top of long-running drought conditions that had settled over much of the region. Then, on Saturday, June 8, 2002, a wisp of smoke arose from an old mining site near Lake George in Park County, about forty-five miles northwest of Colorado Springs. The fire quickly grew in the windy, dry conditions and was named the Hayman Fire, after a nearby ghost town.

The next day, Sunday, June 9, the National Interagency Fire Center issued a Red Flag Warning for the area, with a forecast of extremely low relative humidity and winds of twenty-five to thirty-five miles per hour. Already, the news media were reporting wind gusts of up to sixty miles per hour. Relative humidity was 5 percent and the temperature was 95 degrees, the hottest June 9 in eighty years. On this Red Flag day, despite a strong initial attack by aircraft and ground crews, the Hayman Fire ran seventeen miles. One section of the fire ran a half mile in four minutes. The fire jumped ahead of itself on high winds, creating a spotty pattern of burned areas while other patches of forest remained untouched.

The fire briefly entered the Lost Creek Wilderness, then turned north through Douglas County. It was so hot that it created its own weather, and fire tornadoes swirled in the blaze. Smoke shot up to 15,000 feet, and wind scattered flames in all directions. The smoke and smell of the fire covered a wide area, from Vail, 55 miles northeast; to Burlington, 188 miles east; to Broomfield, 55 miles north; to Walsenburg, 130 miles south. Smoke moved into Wyoming and Nebraska and could even be seen from space. According to the *Denver Post*, ash fell like "plump snowflakes" on Denver.

On Monday, June 10, strong winds again pushed the fire north, and it exploded from 300 acres to more than 75,000 acres in twenty-four hours, coming to within twenty miles of Denver. "It's hard to describe how dangerous a fire like this is," said Lynn Young, a U.S. Forest Service spokesperson for the Rocky Mountain district. "A fire going this fast and going through treetops cannot be stopped. It can't be stopped by a river, it can't be stopped by a subdivision. It's very much out of control. There's nothing to do but get out of the way." In fact, more than 6,000 homes were evacuated in four counties south of Denver.

Fire officials soon designated the Hayman Fire as the nation's top firefighting priority, but several other fires across the state had firefighting resources stretched thin. Air tankers shuffled between the Hayman Fire and the Glenwood Springs Fire, which was also out of control and had forced the evacuation of more than 2,000 people. The situation was chaotic because these wind-driven fires grew and moved so fast. Red Cross shelters would open to help

Firefighters work to save a home from the Hayman Fire. PHOTOGRAPH COURTESY OF THE NATIONAL WEATHER SERVICE.

evacuees but then would just as suddenly close when a fire shifted course, placing the shelter in harm's way.

Governor Bill Owens flew over the Hayman Fire and said, "It looks as if all of Colorado is burning today." He issued a statewide ban against open fires and smoking outdoors, as well as on the sale and use of fireworks. The Pike-San Isabel National Forests closed to all use. County sheriffs throughout the region grappled with evacuation decisions, often avoiding mandatory orders but advising people to be ready to go at a moment's notice. Many residents packed their vehicles and left rather than wait for formal orders.

When Kurt Kyle and his family got the call to "be ready to evacuate" from their home thirty miles south of Denver, they quickly filled a van and a pickup truck with crucial belongings and drove to Kurt's parents' home in Denver. Returning to their home the next day, the Kyles saw that the fire was only five miles away. They loaded televisions, stereos, and a favorite pair of cowboy boots into the van. Mr. Kyle told a reporter, "It's an eerie feeling to think about a fire just over the back ridge. It's hard to think we could leave today, come back tomorrow, and find everything gone." Their neighbors also packed up valuables and keepsakes as they evacuated. Thousands of other families found themselves in the same situation.

By this time, the Hayman Fire had grown to twenty miles long and several miles wide. Its leading edge split into three fingers forking around Cheesman Reservoir. But then, thankfully, the winds died down and humidity rose, and crews were able to make good progress for a week. Another windy period expanded the fire again, but then wetter weather prevailed, and crews had the fire fully contained by July 2 and controlled by July 18.

At the time, the Hayman Fire was the largest and most devastating wildfire in Colorado's history. It burned 138,114 acres and destroyed a total of 600 structures, including one commercial building and 133 homes. A total of 8,000 people were evacuated. More than 2,500 firefighters fought the blaze, at a cost of almost $40 million. Tragically, the fire also led to six fatalities. Ann Dow, who lived south of Florissant, died of an asthma attack when heavy smoke engulfed her house on the evening of July 10.

She collapsed, and paramedics could not save her. Also, five firefighters died on July 21 in a traffic accident on their way from Oregon to help fight the Hayman Fire.

Even in the fire's earliest days, how it started seemed suspicious. A part-time forest technician with the U.S. Forest Service, thirty-eight-year-old Terry Barton, had called in the fire on June 8, reporting that an illegal campfire had escaped its fire ring. But Forest Service special agent Kimberly Jones and other investigators soon realized that "[t]he fire was deliberately set and had been staged to look like an escaped campfire." Jones questioned Barton, who quickly broke down and confessed, claiming she had received an upsetting letter from her estranged husband and had burned it in anger. One of Barton's teenage daughters disputed that story, testifying that a psychologist had told Barton to write about her feelings in a letter and then burn it. In any case, Barton was arrested and charged with arson.

Barton said, "On Saturday, June 8, 2002, I left my home, and my husband handed me a letter. I wasn't speaking with him. And we're going through a divorce. He told me he had burned the divorce papers, earlier in the week when he was in Arkansas. He was supposed to sign the papers. I left for work at 0800 and took the letter with me. The letter was very upsetting to me."

Several years later, as a courtroom witness in a civil case blaming the U.S. Forest Service for the fire, Barton repeated her story. When questioned by detectives, however, she admitted starting the fire. In a written confession, she said that, on her way to work the morning of the fire, she had "decided I wanted to get rid of the letter. I stopped in the road

A seasonal U.S. Forest Service employee, Terry Barton was convicted for causing the Hayman Fire. PHOTOGRAPH BY GEORGE KOCHANEIC, DONATED BY *ROCKY MOUNTAIN NEWS*, COURTESY OF THE DENVER PUBLIC LIBRARY, SPECIAL COLLECTIONS, RMN-044-7625.

and thought, I'm going to get rid of this thing right now." She continued, "I wasn't thinking about the fire ban. I didn't want to start a fire. I thought the campfire ring was a good place to burn the letter. I took it to the campfire ring with matches I had already taken from my purse. I crumpled up the letter and knelt down and put it in the campfire ring and lit it with a match. I watched it till it burned up completely. I thought it was out."

Two investigators doubted her story. They drove to her home in Florissant to speak with John Barton, her estranged husband. He said he had not given her a letter and that he had been sleeping on the porch because she did not want him sleeping inside the house. John Barton went on to say that he didn't see his wife at all on the morning of the fire and that she had spent the night at a friend's house and hadn't been home all that morning.

When confronted with the discrepancies in her story, Terry Barton said that her memory was unclear and that she may have received the letter earlier. She also gave differing accounts of whether she had even read the letter. Further investigation of the fire ring where the letter had supposedly been burned found that there was unburned grass inside the ring and that a stone had been removed from the perimeter, which would've allowed a fire to escape. The investigators suspected that Barton's story was fiction. They also realized how hard it would be to prove that a burned letter had ever existed. Since Terry Barton admitted lighting the match to start the fire, her punishment would have been the same, either way.

A federal grand jury indicted Terry Barton on four felony arson counts. She pleaded guilty to two counts: setting fire to federal forest lands and lying to investigators. For that, she was sentenced to six years in federal prison. U.S. District Judge Richard Matsch refused to impose the $14 million restitution requested by prosecutors. These funds, through the Mandatory Victims Restitution Act, were to be used to reimburse the U.S. Forest Service for revegetating fire-damaged lands. On appeal, in the 10th circuit U.S. Court of Appeals, the restitution funds were granted.

The State of Colorado also sentenced Barton to twelve years in prison to run concurrently with her federal prison sentence. This state-imposed sentence, however, was overturned on appeal because the presiding judge had "the appearance of prejudice;" he had evacuated his home for one night due to smoke from the Hayman Fire. In March 2008, a different judge sentenced Barton to fifteen years on probation and 1,000 hours of community service. She was not sentenced to additional years in prison, but while on probation she still had to pay restitution to the Forest Service and to 1,114 victims listed by the state. The total owed was more than $40 million.

Insurance companies filed a $7 million lawsuit against the government in connection with the Hayman Fire, alleging that Barton was negligent in her duties. In November, the court concluded that the government was not responsible because Barton was not acting as an employee but as an angry spouse.

In June 2008, Terry Barton was released from federal prison in Fort Worth, Texas. She was still under orders to pay restitution but was working part-time and paying only $50 a month toward her debt. Part of her community-service time was spent replanting a section of the forest burned in the fire she set. Her identity was kept secret from others working on the project. She also babysat her grandchildren while her daughter worked.

In August 2018, Barton's sentence was extended another fifteen years in the form of unsupervised probation, which would redirect her legal fees toward restitution. Barton remains on the hook for more than $40 million.

The Hayman fire had huge economic impacts. Many communities in the area rely on tourism and ranching for their livelihoods. Some businesses reported a loss of about half of their typical summer revenue. Ranchers lost feed, fences, and equipment.

Also, beyond the huge costs of fighting the blaze and the loss of burned buildings and equipment, the Hayman Fire burned stands of aspen, spruce, Douglas-fir, and ponderosa pine. An enormous amount of wildlife habitat was lost, including winter roosting sites for bald eagles. The fire consumed all but a few hundred of the 8,000 acres surrounding Cheesman Reservoir, a major Denver watershed. It resulted in the loss of the canopy cover, which directly affects water quality. The nonprofit conservation group American Forests partnered with several local organizations to begin reforesting the Cheesman Reservoir area. They planted 24,000 ponderosa pines, starting in 2004. Additional projects were carried out over the following decade.

Today, the Hayman Restoration Partnership is the largest public-private partnership in Colorado. Volunteers from various community groups have

A collaborative effort aims to revegetate areas burned in the Hayman Fire. PHOTOGRAPH COURTESY OF THE U.S. FOREST SERVICE.

donated thousands of hours to reforestation efforts. The Coalition for the Upper South Platte, Mile High Youth Corps, and Rocky Mountain Field Institute have all been a part of long-term rehabilitation and restoration projects, including installing erosion-control structures and repairing trails and roads. Decades after the Hayman Fire, philanthropic, community, and business partnerships continue to address the destruction from one of Colorado's biggest disasters.

WALDO CANYON FIRE, 2012

Wildfires don't have to burn huge swaths of land to be destructive. The value of the land, the resources on it, and the costs of replacing those resources also come into play. For instance, many grassland fires result in relatively low losses because native grasses are adapted to fire and usually regrow fairly quickly. And human infrastructure tends to be less densely developed in grasslands. In forests, however, the economic value of timber can be high, and there may be more homes, resorts, campgrounds, and other development. When wildfires burn close to towns and cities—in what experts call the wildland-urban interface—resource and monetary losses can skyrocket.

One of Colorado's more destructive wildfires started on Saturday, June 23, 2012, in Waldo Canyon, about four miles northwest of Colorado Springs. Although this fire burned only a little more than 18,000 acres and was contained within seventeen days, it was deadly and extremely costly.

The Waldo Canyon Fire began at about noon as a brush fire in Pike National Forest and was first spotted by a group of cyclists on mountain bikes on Rampart Range Road. Erratic winds pushed it in multiple directions, and the fire spread quickly. The Colorado Springs Fire Department requested air support at 12:24 P.M. By 3 P.M., the fire had grown to 600 acres and was heading toward the small towns of Chipita Park, Green Mountain Falls, and Cascade along U.S. Highway 24 between Woodland Park and Manitou Springs. It also spread toward Manitou Springs and Colorado Springs. Seeing the smoke and assessing the windy conditions, some residents began to evacuate.

Colorado Springs requested help from fire departments in Stratmoor Hills, Cheyenne Mountain Air Force Station, Cimarron Hills, and Peterson Air Force Base. A crew began to cut a firebreak above Cedar Heights, but a conventional firebreak won't do much to stop a crown fire, and this one was burning through treetops seven stories high. Firefighters were hampered by high temperatures, low humidity, and strong winds.

On June 25, the fire jumped Rampart Ridge Road and quickly spread into Queens Canyon, west of Glen Eyrie Conference Center, where the steep topography made it hard for firefighters. About noon that day, two aircraft from Peterson Air Force Base and two from Wyoming made their first retardant drops on the blaze. The next day, Colorado Springs set a record high temperature of 101 degrees F. The fire continued to expand in Queens Canyon and went down the slope and into the neighborhoods of Mountain Shadows, Oak Valley Ranch, and Peregrine. Driven by its own sixty-five-mile-per-hour winds, the fire chewed through residential areas house by house.

Emergency calls went out to the Mountain Shadows neighborhood during rush hour, when cell networks were in heavy use. Many of these emergency calls went to voicemail, fax machines, and discontinued phone numbers. Thousands of people were headed home from work, calling each other and phoning home. About 20,000 calls could not be completed because of busy circuits. Two residents, seventy-four-year-old William Everett and his wife, Barbara, seventy-three, did not receive a warning call. Their phones were not linked to the county's alert system, and they succumbed to smoke and flames as they tried to flee their burning home.

By late afternoon on Tuesday, June 26, 7,000 residents of North Mountain Shadows and Peregrine were ordered to evacuate as the fire was racing toward the subdivisions. This evacuation was in addition to 4,825 residents evacuated earlier. More than 1,000 firefighters were attacking the blaze. Rich Harvey, Waldo Canyon incident commander, said that, in addition to firefighters and emergency workers, "We have resources on this fire from an alphabet soup of agencies. Our resources have wheels, they have tracks, they have rotors, they have wings."

By 9 P.M. Tuesday, evacuation orders had gone out to 32,000 residents. The Red Cross shelter at Cheyenne Mountain was taking in people and small, caged pets, while the Penrose Equestrian Center offered to shelter horses and other livestock.

By that evening, the fire had engulfed many homes and other structures, including the landmark Flying W Ranch. Within one twelve-hour span,

A Sikorsky S-64 helicopter drops water on the Waldo Canyon Fire. PHOTOGRAPH BY SERGEANT JEREMY LOCK, COURTESY OF THE U.S. AIR FORCE.

346 homes had burned to the ground in western Colorado Springs and hundreds more were damaged. The Colorado Springs *Gazette* and *Denver Post* both ran an aerial photograph showing, street by street, which areas had burned, and that was how many residents learned that their homes were gone. By the end of the night, fire crews had achieved only 15 percent containment of the Waldo Canyon Fire.

From California, the Vandenberg Air Force Base Hot Shots arrived in Colorado Springs and helped limit the eastward movement of the fire. Some firefighters had already been on duty for thirty-six hours and had suffered minor injuries as well as fatigue. At the height of the fire, 1,500 firefighters bivouacked at the Holmes Middle School near Garden of the Gods. Hundreds of grateful people lined the streets to cheer firefighters as they came off their shifts.

On June 29, President Barack Obama visited the Waldo Canyon Fire and declared it a federal disaster. He visited the Mountain Shadows neighborhood, a fire station, and a Red Cross evacuation shelter. As he toured the burned neighborhood southwest of the U.S. Air Force Academy, the president saw houses razed to the ground, melted pipes spewing water, and burned-out cars in driveways. He said, "We've got to make sure that we have each other's backs. And that spirit is what you're seeing in terms of volunteers, in terms of firefighters, in terms of government officials. Everybody is pulling together to try to deal with this situation."

The emergency room staff of the Memorial Health System treated adults and children with breathing problems due to the heavy smoke. Help was also provided by University of Colorado Health and the Children's Hospital in Aurora.

By July 5, the fire was 90 percent contained. But burglars had hit thirty-seven of the evacuated homes, and authorities were offering $50,000 for information on the culprits. The National Guard was called in to patrol and protect evacuated areas. Finally, on July 10, the Waldo Canyon Fire was declared 100 percent contained.

In less than three weeks, this fire had killed two people, burned twenty square miles, and destroyed 346 homes. It forced the closure of U.S. Highway 24, a major east-west road. The Waldo Canyon Fire was also one

NASA's Terra satellite captured this image of the Waldo Canyon burn scar (dark colored) against the lighter hue of vegetation and development. PHOTOGRAPH COURTESY OF THE NATIONAL AERONAUTICS AND SPACE ADMINISTRATION.

of the costliest in Colorado's history. It cost $15 million to $20 million to fight and contain. Insurance claims totaled more than $453.7 million.

But the disaster wasn't over. Much of the burned national forest lands were as barren as the moon. Without trees and other vegetation to stabilize soils on steep mountain slopes, future rains and snowmelt could bring floods and mudslides.

In response, the U.S. Forest Service began cleaning culverts and putting up warning signs in slide-prone areas. Colorado Springs Utilities spent more than $8 million to repair a damaged pipeline, an access road, and sediment-containment basins. Volunteers, including Air Force Academy cadets, built retention ponds to catch storm runoff and sediment. The city also began planning to mulch bare slopes, build retaining walls, and increase the size of drainage structures, with many projects slated to begin in 2013.

Colorado Springs also began rebuilding in burned-out neighborhoods. Recognizing the historical significance of the fire, the Colorado Springs

Pioneers Museum asked citizens to record what had happened to them and also collected artifacts. These were gathered into an exhibit called "From the Ashes: The Waldo Canyon Fire."

At one point during the fire, the little tourist town of Manitou Springs had been under an evacuation order. Residents were relieved when winds shifted and their town was spared. But the spring and summer of 2013 brought heavy rains, and then floods and debris flows. Between July 1 and the end of August, four separate floods struck Manitou Springs. The worst of these occurred on August 9, 2013, when rains drenched the fire-blackened slopes and canyons above town. A flash flood of mud, rocks, and debris roared into town.

Bree Jensen, a Manitou Springs resident, told a *Los Angeles Times* reporter, "You could hear the rumbling before you saw it. It was like this enormous black wall of water." Within minutes, the debris-laden water swept down Canyon Avenue four feet deep, upending cars and splintering buildings. Another resident, Erin Collyer, tried to outrun the flood. She was swept up in the water but lashed her daypack straps to a pole and hung on until she was able to reach safety. Another resident, John Collins, died after being buried under the mud and debris. It is not known whether he was fleeing on foot or had been swept from his car, which was uncovered a short distance from his body. Six homes were lost in the mudflow, and residents were warned not to rebuild in the same area.

Lynn Highland, coordinator of the U.S. Geological Survey National Landslide Information Center in Golden, Colorado, said, "While these debris flows are not unprecedented in Colorado, it's the frequency that is increasing." Burned landscapes are especially vulnerable. Manitou Springs would be at risk for repeat floods for up to ten years, until the landscape recovers, Highland said.

Investigators concluded that the Waldo Canyon Fire was human-caused, but they could not determine precisely how it started. Almost exactly one year later, on June 11, 2013, similar hot, dry, windy conditions fanned another human-caused fire in the Black Forest community northeast of Colorado Springs. That fire also killed two people and eclipsed Waldo Canyon, destroying 486 homes.

Despite the devastation from the Waldo Canyon Fire, the U.S. Forest Service reported that aspen began to sprout a month after the fire. Wildlife, including bighorn sheep, also returned.

———

For everyone, 2020 was a year to remember because of the COVID-19 pandemic that disrupted lives throughout the world. On a smaller scale but still filled with drama, 2020 was a year to remember because of huge wildfires that burned out of control in many western states. That was certainly true for Colorado, where more than 1,000 wildfires burned that year. Up to that time, the biggest wildfire to ever occur in the state happened in 2002. But suddenly, in 2020, three wildfires—Pine Gulch, Cameron Peak, and East Troublesome—each surpassed the previous record.

PINE GULCH FIRE, 2020

Triple smoke plumes from the Pine Gulch Fire coalesce into one cloud on August 15, 2020. PHOTOGRAPH BY JIM CALDWELL, COURTESY OF THE GRAND JUNCTION FIELD OFFICE, U.S.BUREAU OF LAND MANAGEMENT.

A lightning strike ignited the Pine Gulch Fire on July 31, 2020. It was reported at about 5:15 P.M. on Bureau of Land Management land in a remote area about eighteen miles north of Grand Junction. In the first twenty-four hours, the fire grew to 280 acres, consuming grass and sagebrush, as well as pinyon, juniper, and fir trees. Initial attack crews arrived on foot and were aided by airplanes and helicopters dropping water and retardant on the flames. But the rugged terrain and dry conditions hampered efforts to contain the fire. By August 2, the fire had burned 1,400 acres and had spread north onto private land. In this steep, remote, and drought-stricken area, the fire burned for weeks. The smoke plume could be seen from Grand Junction.

Winds of up to forty miles per hour hit the area during a thunderstorm the night of August 18, and the fire grew by more than 30,000 acres. Firefighters used bulldozers to create firebreaks, and hand crews did their best to protect homes and outbuildings.

With the sudden explosion in the fire's size, local residents were evacuated, and Governor Jared Polis declared a state of emergency. This allowed agencies to coordinate and make resources available for fire suppression, response, and recovery efforts. Polis also activated the National Guard to assist the state emergency-operations center and incident commanders.

Crews battle the Pine Gulch Fire. PHOTOGRAPH COURTESY OF THE GRAND JUNCTION FIELD OFFICE, U.S. BUREAU OF LAND MANAGEMENT.

The fire brought heavy smoke to the Western Slope. On some mornings, ash collected in layers on windowsills and windshields, and the smoke was so thick it obscured the Book Cliffs on Grand Junction's northern edge. Health advisories were issued locally and in nearby towns.

On August 27, 2020, the Pine Gulch Fire, which was now burning in both Mesa and Garfield Counties, became the largest wildfire in Colorado history, surpassing the 2002 Hayman Fire. As the fire kept growing in size, residents on its northwest edge received evacuation notices. Others remained on pre-evacuation alert. The Pine Gulch Fire was not 100 percent contained until September 23, 2020. By then, it had burned 139,007 acres.

CAMERON PEAK FIRE, 2020

On August 13, 2020, a wildfire was reported northwest of Chambers Lake in the Roosevelt National Forest, about forty miles west of Fort Collins. The blaze grew rapidly, fueled by extremely dry conditions and strong winds. The U.S. Forest Service also noted that "[a] major contributing factor to the large fire growth was the tremendous amount of beetle kill trees and the drought-stricken ponderosa pine, Engelmann spruce, and mixed conifer stands available as fuel."

An operator uses a bulldozer to build a fire line on the Cameron Peak Fire. PHOTOGRAPH COURTESY OF THE ARAPAHO-ROOSEVELT NATIONAL FOREST.

The fire, now known as the Cameron Peak Fire, quickly grew to 10,867 acres and, driven by seventy-mile-per-hour wind gusts, jumped to the south side of Colorado Highway 14 and the Cache la Poudre River. On August 21, the Larimer County sheriff ordered mandatory and immediate evacuation of area residences and businesses, saying that danger was imminent. More evacuations were issued over the coming weeks. (It was not until November 2 that all evacuation notices from the Cameron Peak Fire were lifted.)

Downwind of the fire, people lived with hazy skies and the strong smell of smoke. Outdoor lights, set to turn on automatically at dusk, came on by

A slurry bomber drops retardant on the Cameron Peak Fire. PHOTOGRAPH COURTESY OF THE ARAPAHO-ROOSEVELT NATIONAL FOREST.

early afternoon. Sometimes the sky glowed a brilliant orange. Unhealthy air quality alerts became common in Front Range communities. These conditions prevailed through much of September and October of 2020.

By October 14, a mere seven weeks after the Pine Gulch Fire had taken the title of the largest fire in Colorado history, the Cameron Peak Fire surpassed it. Then, on October 16, gusts as high as seventy-six miles per hour drove the fire onto new ground, pushing back firefighting crews. On October 18, the Cameron Peak Fire became the first in Colorado history to burn more than 200,000 acres. The fire's reach included 30,000 acres within Rocky Mountain National Park.

Fortunately, starting on October 24, temperatures plummeted and more than a foot of snow fell on the fire over several days. "It was a much-needed reprieve for the firefighters," said David Wolf, fire chief for the Estes Valley Fire Protection District. While the snow slowed the growth of the fire, it also severely limited firefighter access to the area. Some of the firefighting equipment did not work well in the extremely cold weather. Chief Wolf added, "It seems like the snow is going to do some really good things for us in the light fuels like grass and meadows, but up in the timber we're concerned that the fire will be able to come back to life after a couple of days of warming, possibly as early as late this week." Wolf was right—that's exactly what happened. The snow did not smother the fire and put it out. But crews used the lull to assess damage to structures and begin notifying residents about the status of their homes. In all, the Cameron Peak Fire destroyed 224 homes and 220 outbuildings.

Remarkably, no deaths were attributed to the fire. Larimer County Sheriff Justin Smith said "I am so proud of the deputies, firefighters, and a variety of other officers from many other law enforcement agencies who heroically evacuated thousands and thousands of people and made sure that no one felt the pain of losing a loved one to this fire."

On November 10, 2020, officials declared the Cameron Peak Fire 100 percent contained. It had burned 208,913 acres and rewritten the history books.

EAST TROUBLESOME FIRE, 2020

Another wildfire sparked on October 14, 2020, northeast of Kremmling. The East Troublesome Fire (named for the East Fork of Troublesome Creek near its starting point) was fueled by the same conditions that fed the Cameron Peak Fire: hot, dry weather, high winds, and ample fuel in the form of drought-weakened and beetle-killed trees.

Then, on the afternoon of October 21, winds increased, with gusts up to 100 miles per hour, driving the fire east. It jumped Colorado Highway 125 and ran toward Lake Granby, the town of Grand Lake, and the west side of Rocky Mountain National Park. By the afternoon of the next day, October 22, the fire had exploded from 18,550 acres to 187,964 acres, threatening more than 7,000 homes and businesses. More than 35,000 people fled under mandatory-evacuation orders. As it grew, the East Troublesome Fire spread toward the Cameron Peak Fire, coming within ten miles, and officials worried that the two fires might merge.

Within Rocky Mountain National Park, the East Troublesome Fire split into two prongs. During the night, one prong hopped over the Continental Divide and moved east along the Big Thompson River, with spot fires on Beaver Mountain and in Moraine Park. The park's fire management officer, Mike Lewelling, recalled, "We had met briefly at midnight, then about 5:30 A.M. I get a call from the National Weather Service, and they said that weather satellites were picking up heat signatures from east of the

Continental Divide. The guy told me it must be significant because their satellite is over the equator."

That big run of flames destroyed several historic buildings, including the Onahu Lodge and the Green Mountain Cabins along Trail Ridge Road in the Kawuneeche Valley. The park also lost the Trails and Tack Barn, the Grand Lake entrance station office, and the garage at Trail River Ranch, where historical materials were stored. Crews had tried to protect the buildings, but the fire hit so fast that they barely had time to save themselves. They escaped by driving east on Trail Ridge Road, eight minutes ahead of the flames, with trees falling around them in the hurricane-force winds.

East of the Divide, the fire destroyed the oldest structure in the park, the Fern Lake Backcountry Patrol Cabin, which had been built in 1925. "In ninety-five years, countless rangers, wilderness crews, trails crews, biologists, and search and rescue operations have been based and supported out of this cabin," said park Superintendent Darla Sidles.

With high winds driving a crown fire down Forest Canyon and spot fires blooming into full-grown conflagrations, officials decided to evacuate Estes Park. More than 10,000 people packed up and drove east to the plains. Hot-shot crews made a last stand in Beaver Meadows, setting backfires in fifty-mile-per-hour winds, even as the main blaze raced toward them across the meadow. Lewelling, the fire manager, said, "On the morning of October 23, I was absolutely sure we were going to see Estes burn."

But the weather lent a helping hand. The winds eased, and a heavy fog bank formed over the east side of the peaks. The cooler, damp air tamped down the worst of the flames. Then, overnight between October 24 and 25, one to two feet of snow fell. The fire continued to smolder, but the snow sapped its strength. By November 30, the fire was fully contained.

The East Troublesome Fire burned a total of 193,812 acres and destroyed 366 homes and 214 outbuildings. Of course, damage was not confined to buildings and historical artifacts. The fire devastated ponderosa-pine woodlands, upland meadows, and conifer forests choked with beetle-killed trees. It also burned through wetlands, riparian areas, and groves of aspen. Recovery from such a fire would take time. Holding out hope, Superintendent Sidles said, "The natural resources will recover with new life sprouting up in the fire's footprint, and we will move forward and continue to do our best and manage Rocky Mountain National Park to preserve the natural and cultural resources for the enjoyment, education, and inspiration of this and future generations."

Tens of thousands of people fled their homes as the East Troublesome Fire approached, but one couple declined to leave. Lyle and Marilyn Hileman, both in their eighties, had met in high school, married, and long ago honeymooned in Grand Lake. After Lyle's career as a construction contractor and Denver firefighter and Marilyn's as a mental-health worker at Fort Logan, they had returned to Grand Lake to build a rambling, two-story home for their retirement. On the night of the fire's big run, they knew it was coming but chose to remain, sheltering in their basement. Their remains were later found in the rubble.

The terrible wildfire season of 2020 has clear links to climate change. Jennifer Balch, director of Earth Lab at the University of Colorado Boulder, points to several trends leading to longer fire seasons with more intense wildfires. First, decades of warmer, drier, shorter winters have allowed mountain pine beetles to infest larger tracts of forest. Drought conditions have stressed the trees, leaving them more susceptible to the beetles. Continued drought and high temperatures also favor big, hot wildfires. At the same time, more people are building homes on forest lands. Balch said, "If I had a panic button, I would push it—we have put millions of homes in harm's way across the western U.S."

MARSHALL FIRE, 2021

It looked as if 2021 would pass without setting any wildfire records in Colorado, but on the next-to-last day, December 30, record-breaking drought conditions and hurricane-force winds conspired to close the year in a devastating way. On that date, sometime before noon, a grass fire ignited just southeast of Boulder near the junction of Marshall Road and South Foothills Highway (Colorado Highway 93). Thanks to months of extremely dry weather and a lack of snow, several small grass fires had broken out during the preceding week, and another fire sparked north of

Boulder the morning of the 30th, but these were all extinguished without much difficulty.

The fire southeast of Boulder was different. Gale-force winds roared out of the mountains and fanned the flames, sending embers flying eastward. By 3 P.M., a mandatory evacuation had been issued for 32,000 residents in the towns of Superior and Louisville. Many people had only minutes to leave their homes, as soot and grit filled the air. Sheriff's deputies issuing evacuation warnings said the flames came so quickly that they, too, were caught in the rush to escape. Some reported that the decals on their patrol cars blistered from the intense heat. Within those first three hours of the blaze, more than 500 homes were destroyed.

Officials had issued a Red Flag No-Burn alert and a high-wind warning for Boulder County that morning as 30- to 50-mile-per-hour winds buffeted the area. Then the wind speed increased, with gusts up to 115 miles per hour at nearby Rocky Flats. The flames raced across drought-stressed grasslands and brushy fields, quickly reaching Superior and Louisville. There, whipped by frenzied winds, flames leapt from house to house. One front of the fire engulfed the Sagamore subdivision in Superior, spreading into an adjacent shopping center and Old Town.

Local fire departments rushed to the scene, but they were helpless in the face of violent winds. The high winds also grounded all aircraft, so water and retardant drops were not an option.

The Marshall Fire burns through a neighborhood in Boulder County. PHOTOGRAPH COURTESY OF SOUTH METRO FIRE DEPARTMENT, BOULDER COUNTY.

It was not until about 7 P.M. on December 30 when the high winds finally eased to twenty miles per hour. Finally, firefighters could attack the fire more effectively. Their efforts were helped greatly as snow began to fall in Boulder County the next day.

On New Year's Day, hot spots still smoldered, but most of the fires were out and the full extent of the devastation could be seen. Boulder County Sheriff Joe Pelle later announced that the fire had destroyed 1,084 homes and damaged another 149. Seven business buildings were a total loss and 30 more were damaged. Among those, the Element Hotel in Superior had burned to the ground, and nearby Target and Costco stores and a Tesla dealership had sustained considerable damage.

On the morning of the fire, Rex and Barba Hickman fled their Louisville home of twenty-three years with nothing more than their dog, iPads, and the clothes on their backs. They returned several days later to find a pile of ashes and debris. "There's a numbness that hits you first," Rex Hickman said. "The real pain is going to sink in over time."

That pain was doubled for Wayne and Samantha Shelnutt of Superior. Their home was destroyed when the fire gutted the Sagamore subdivision, and their business, Wayne's Smoke Shack, a barbecue restaurant in the same shopping center as the singed Target and Costco, suffered severe soot and smoke damage. "Literally everything in there is covered in toxic smoke and soot," Wayne Shelnutt said. "It might be a total loss on every piece of equipment that I have." Abruptly becoming homeless and unemployed on the same day would have been challenging enough, but Samantha was also seven months pregnant. Fortunately, the couple had been eager supporters of the community, providing meals for frontline workers during the pandemic. So the community stepped up and helped the Shelnutts with complimentary lodging, meals, and clothes. The couple plans to reopen the restaurant, but Wayne Shelnutt figured it might take six months to a year to get it back up and running.

On December 31, Governor Jared Polis surveyed the approximately ten square miles of wildfire devastation from a helicopter. Speaking to the media, he said, "I know this is a hard time in your life if you've lost everything or you don't even know what you lost. A few days ago you were

Surveying the damage from a helicopter, Governor Jared Polis saw firsthand the devastation caused by the Marshall Fire. PHOTOGRAPH BY JARED POLIS, COURTESY OF THE OFFICE OF THE GOVERNOR.

celebrating Christmas at home and hanging your stockings and now home and hearth have been destroyed." He also declared a state of emergency, and President Joe Biden approved an expedited national emergency declaration to help victims obtain aid prior to the final assessment of the costs of this fire. Preliminary estimates peg losses at more than $513 million, making the Marshall Fire the costliest disaster to date in Colorado history. Miraculously, only a handful of people were injured, including one firefighter. But six days after the blaze, two people remained missing: ninety-one-year-old Edna "Nadine" Turnbull of Superior and sixty-nine-year-old Robert Sharpe, who lived on Marshall Road. Searchers later found Sharpe's body in the rubble of his home.

Although officials initially suspected downed power lines as the ignition source of the Marshall Fire, investigators said they've found no downed lines, and the fire's cause remains under investigation.

SOURCES

Hayman Fire, 2002

Booth, William, and Gerard Wright. "After Forester's Arrest, Disbelief and Anger." *Washington Post*, June 18, 2002.

Cart, Julie. "Raging fire bears down on Denver." *Los Angeles Times*, June 11, 2002.

Graham, Russell T., ed. *Hayman Fire Case Study*. Ogden, Utah, U.S. Department of Agriculture Forest Service, Rocky Mountain Research Station, GTR-114, 2003.

Ingold, John. "Decades after Hayman fire, questions linger over fire's start." *Denver Post*, June 2, 2012.

Janofsky, Michael. "Fires from Hell, Views from Heaven." *The New York Times*, June 12, 2002.

McHugh, Charles W., and Paul Gleason. "Part 5: Fire Suppression Activities." *Hayman Fire Case Study*, USDA Forest Service General Technical Report RMRS-GTR-114, 2003.

Sink, Mindy. "Added Term in Forest Fire." *The New York Times*, March 6, 2003.

Waldo Canyon Fire, 2012

Brown, Jennifer. "Waldo Canyon fire evacuation warnings failed to reach thousands." *Denver Post*, July 10, 2012.

Deam, Jenny. "A year after Waldo Canyon fire, Colorado town contends with flooding." *Los Angeles Times*, August 29, 2013.

Gabbert, Bill. "President Obama visits the Waldo Canyon Fire." *Wildfire Today*, June 29, 2012.

Laden, Rich. "Waldo Canyon Fire: Flying W Ranch burns to ground." Colorado Springs *Gazette*, June 26, 2012.

Lee, Kurtis. "Waldo Canyon fire forces 11,000 people from their homes." *Denver Post*, June 24, 2012.

Meyer, Jeremy P. "Coroner officially IDs victims of Waldo Canyon fire." *Denver Post*, October 1, 2012.

Nelson, Laura J. "Colorado's most destructive fire ever, Waldo Canyon is contained." *Los Angeles Times*, July 11, 2012.

Stephens, Bob. "Looming danger: Burned slopes increase risk of flash floods." Colorado Springs *Gazette*, January 26, 2013.

"Waldo Canyon Fire Burns Homes, 32,000 Ordered to Evacuate." News 4 CBS, Denver, June 26, 2012.

Pine Gulch Fire, 2020

Pine Gulch Fire. Inciweb Incident Information System, last modified June 21, 2021.

Sieg, Stina. "Pine Gulch Fire is Now the Largest in Colorado History." CPR News, August 27, 2020.

Tabachnik, Sam. "Colorado wildfire update: Latest on the Pine Gulch, Grizzly Creek, Cameron Peak, and Williams Fork fires." *Denver Post*, August 22, 2020.

Cameron Peak Fire, 2020

Associated Press. "Breaking records, Colorado wildfires drag on later than normal." *Los Angeles Times*, October 23, 2020.

Miller, Blair. "Sheriff's Office: 469 structures damaged or destroyed in Cameron Peak Fire, including 42 primary homes." KOAA News 5, November 7, 2020.

East Troublesome Fire, 2020

Blumhardt, Miles. "Rocky Mountain National Park official 'was absolutely sure' Estes Park would burn in 2020 fire." Fort Collins *Coloradoan*, June 18, 2021.

East Troublesome Fire. Inciweb Incident Information System, last modified June 21, 2021.

Leary, Jamie. "Family believes grandparents died near Grand Lake in East Troublesome fire." CBS News 4, Denver, October 23, 2020.

Navarro, Natalia V. "Snow Blankets Cameron Peak and East Troublesome Fires as Crews Regroup." CPR News, October 26, 2020.

Worthington, Danika. "Rocky Mountain National Park loses several historic structures in East Troublesome fire." *Denver Post*, November 6, 2020.

Marshall Fire, 2021

"2 missing, 991 homes destroyed in Marshall Fire." NBC 9 News, Denver, January 1, 2022.

Byars, Mitchell. "'A force of nature': Marshall Fire grows to 1,600 acres, forces evacuation of Superior, Louisville, Broomfield." *Greeley Tribune*, December 30, 2021.

"Family anxious to find missing Edna 'Nadine' Turnbull following Marshall Fire." CBS 4 News, Denver, January 2, 2022.

Gabbert, Bill. "Wind-driven wildfire burns hundreds of homes near Boulder, Colorado." Wildfire Today, December 30, 2021.

McKee, Spencer. "How much damage was done by the Marshall Fire in Boulder County, Colorado?" *OutThere Colorado*, January 3, 2022.

Michels, Ashley. "Expecting Superior couple loses both home and business in Marshall Fire." Fox 31, Denver, January 5, 2022.

Peipert, Thomas. "2 still missing in Marshall Fire; cause under investigation." Associated Press, in the *Colorado Sun*, January 3, 2022.

INDEX

Page numbers in **bold** indicate images.

ABOUT THE AUTHOR

PHYLLIS J. PERRY WAS BORN IN Grass Valley, a small gold-mining town in Northern California. She earned a BA in English literature with a minor in history at the University of California, Berkeley. She taught elementary school in the Mount Diablo Unified School District and earned a master's degree in education from San Francisco State University. During this time, she experienced the tremors of two earthquakes. Perry moved with her husband, David, and two daughters to Long Beach, where David taught at Long Beach State University and Phyllis taught part-time at Golden West Junior College.

Perry and her family eventually moved to Boulder, Colorado, where her husband joined the faculty at the University of Colorado. She earned her doctorate in education there and then served for twenty years in the Boulder Valley Schools as a teacher, school principal, and director of a program for talented and gifted students. Perry took early retirement to write full-time. She is an award-winning author of fiction and nonfiction for both children and adults and is a member of the Colorado Authors' League and the Society of Children's Book Writers and Illustrators. Perry has written 95 books. In 2017, she received the Lifetime Achievement Award from the Colorado Authors' League.

Perry welcomes comments and can be reached through her website at www.phyllisjperry.com.

MORE GREAT BOOKS FROM

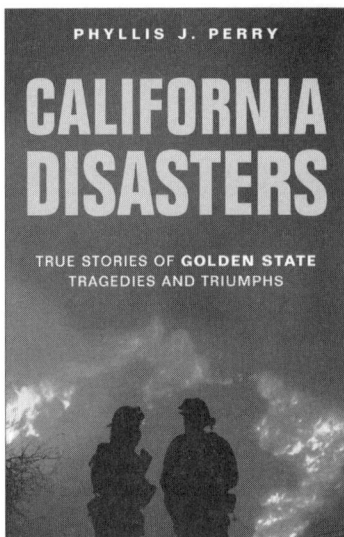

FARCOUNTRY
PRESS

CALIFORNIA DISASTERS:
TRUE STORIES OF GOLDEN STATE
TRAGEDIES AND TRIUMPHS

By Phyllis J. Perry

California Disasters highlights some of the major such events occurring in the state over the last two hundred years. Some disasters are man-made, and others are the result of the forces of nature, such as the snow-trapped Donner Party of 1846 or the unforgettable fire and earthquake of 1906 in San Francisco and the Bay Area.

MONTANA DISASTERS:
TRUE STORIES OF TREASURE STATE
TRAGEDIES AND TRIUMPHS

By Butch Larcomb

In Montana Disasters, fourth-generation Montanan and long-time journalist Butch Larcombe chronicles the explosions, fires, floods, earthquakes, avalanches, train wrecks, airplane crashes, and other major tragedies spanning more than a century.

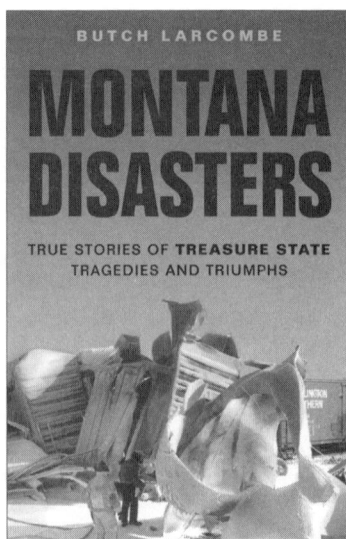

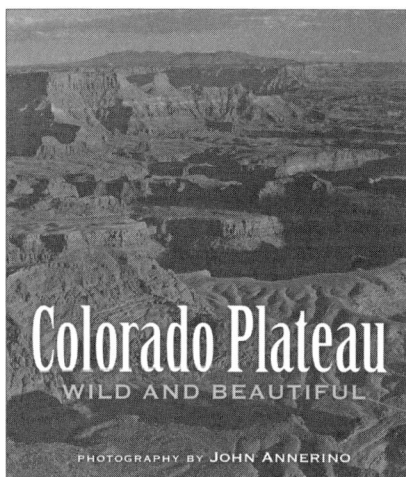

COLORADO PLATEAU:
WILD AND BEAUTIFUL

Photography by John Annerino

Discover the adventure and mystery of the Colorado Plateau along sheer cliffs, through white-water rapids, and among ancient dwellings.

COLORADO:
WILD AND BEAUTIFUL

Photography and text by Glenn Randall

From 14,000-foot peaks to deep and sinuous canyons, Randall presents a joyous celebration of a unique state.

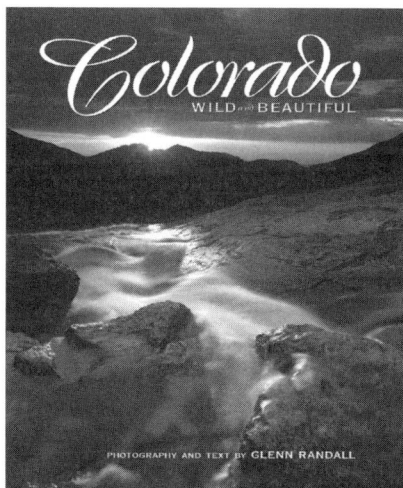

COLORADO:
WILDLIFE PORTFOLIO

Photography and text by Lee Kline
Foreword by Chris Madson, editor of Wyoming Wildlife *magazine*

A true photographic treasure, pairing spectacular images of wildlife with fascinating and informative captions.

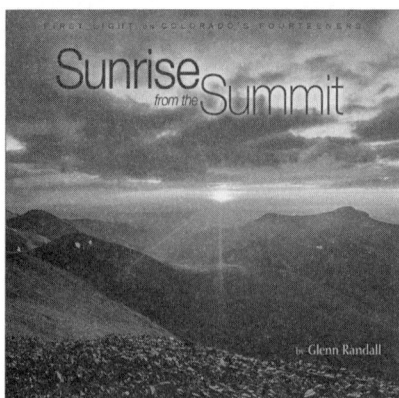